A HERO ALL HIS LIFE

Merlyn, Mickey Jr., David, and Dan Mantle

with MICKEY HERSKOWITZ

A Memoir by the Mantle Family

HarperCollins*Publishers*

HarperCollins books may be purchased for educational, business, or sales promotional use. For information please write: Special Markets Department, HarperCollins Publishers, Inc., 10 East 53rd Street, New York, NY 10022.

FIRST EDITION

Designed by Alma Hochhauser Orenstein

Library of Congress Cataloging-in-Publication Data

A hero all his life / Merlyn Mantle . . . [et al.]. — 1st ed.
    p. cm.
   Includes index.
   ISBN 0-06-018363-2
   1. Mantle, Mickey, 1931– . 2. Baseball players—United States—Biography. 3. Mantle, Merlyn. 4. Baseball players' spouses—United States—Biography. 5. New York Yankees (Baseball team)—History. I. Mantle, Merlyn.
   GV865.M33H46   1996
   796.357'092—dc20
   [B]   96-24774

96 97 98 99 00 ❖/RRD 10 9 8 7 6 5 4 3 2 1

To Mick and Billy—peace and love

Contents

Photographs follow page 118.

Acknowledgments

THIS BOOK WAS A FAMILY CHALLENGE BECAUSE NEARLY all of it came out of the experiences we had endured and shared and, in some cases, were reluctant to relive. We probably ought to begin by thanking the staff at the Betty Ford Center and Merlyn's friends in her twelve-step program for helping us attain the clear heads that were essential to the task.

But in the process of completing the book itself, the Mantle family had the help of unsung teammates. This is fitting, because Mick, who is at the center of our story and our lives, was consistent in his desire to be remembered as a team player.

As always, Roy True gave us his wise and patient advice. Kathy Hampton helped us juggle the schedule and the networking, with the assistance of Pat Dean.

To Gladys Carr, HarperCollins vice president and associate publisher, who believed in the importance of this book, and to editor Cynthia Vail Barrett and associate editor Elissa Mandy Altman, who guided us through it, we are sincerely indebted.

The Mick

It has been this way most of my life: If I said or did something wrong, the people who might have suffered for it would worry about my feelings being hurt. Even eight-year-olds made excuses for me.

Chapter 1

Extra Innings

SOMETIMES WHEN I READ STORIES ABOUT MY CAREER, or look at old film clips of me circling the bases, it's as if these things happened to someone else.

Sometimes when people talk to me about a game they saw or a home run I hit, it is all a blur to me. When I can't remember, I get frustrated and angry. I hate getting older, and I hate knowing all the ways I screwed up.

These are part of the reasons I didn't intend to ever write another book. Writing a book has never been natural to me; I mean, I'm not comfortable telling a writer things about myself that I'm not ready to talk about.

I felt that way my whole life, but now I am ready to talk about being an alcoholic. I don't think I was ever really nervous on a baseball field, in any league, in any situation. But I thought I might pass out the first time I stood up in a meeting at the Betty Ford Center and said, "I'm Mick and I'm an alcoholic."

I don't have any problem saying those words here, now, because it took me a lot of years to be honest with people, including myself. I wish I had said it in 1969, when my thirst went from steady to almost nonstop.

So I was in a different frame of mind when my friend and lawyer, Roy True, asked me to write a book with my family, and to tell our story about what alcohol did to each of us. I'm doing this because my sons want to do it and because I think I owe it to people for all the support I received when I went into treatment to stop my drinking.

People have written me, and stopped me in person, and told me that when I got help they decided they could get sober, too. If our story can help other families to avoid alcoholism or get help for themselves, then this will be a book I will take pride in. But I promise, this will be my last book.

I don't make jokes or laugh anymore about drinking. I no longer try to separate the baseball part of my life from the struggles I've had outside it. I am still getting used to the fact that when I admitted I was a drunk and had been one for decades, I received letters by the thousands. By mail and in public, people praised me, encouraged me, and identified with me. I was really touched by those letters, and many of them made me cry. I was afraid people would think less of me.

Instead, they said they were glad I had the courage to confront my alcohol abuse. One of these days, I would like somebody to publish these letters.* They really helped me and I think they could inspire others also.

---

*Somebody did. HarperCollins published *Letters to Mickey* in the fall of 1995.

But the truth is, I really didn't think I deserved their sympathy or admiration. I appreciated it—but I'm ashamed that I let my drinking blur my memory and blur my life like it has. I missed so much because of alcohol.

The doctors told me if I didn't stop, the next drink could kill me. I'd been told before that my drinking was ruining my liver, but just before I went to get help, the stomach pains and memory loss were so bad that when the doctor told me again, I paid attention.

How did I get this way? Hell, I don't know. It just happened.

I don't want this to sound like an excuse, but I was a product of my times, and those were the best of times to be a baseball player—not because of the money, which was nothing compared to today, but because of the game. It was America's game. The Yankees were America's team. We didn't play for the paycheck. We played because we loved to play, and we played to win. That's just the way it was. You played the game, you won or lost, and then you headed for the bars, where we replayed the games.

Temptations were everywhere. Fans would buy us drinks, girls would hang around to meet us, and, at least when we were on the road, boredom was an enemy. In those days, how well you could hold your liquor was, for many of us, a measure of being a man. At the ballpark, you belted them out. At the bar, you belted them down.

Bobby Layne was a friend of mine. Bobby was the great quarterback for the Pittsburgh Steelers and the Detroit Lions. Bobby's creed was, "Live fast, die young, leave a handsome corpse." Bobby would refer to a "fast forty," meaning years.

He had a reputation for drinking much like the one I got after several seasons. Surprisingly, only a few of my nighttime escapades made it into print in New York, or in other cities where we played. In those days there was an unwritten rule among the baseball reporters: If the way you spent your free time didn't hurt the club, then it was off the record.

I can remember only one time when drinking affected my game. I had partied so late, and had such a bad hangover, that Casey Stengel decided to hold me out of the game. "You look like hell," he said. "Take the day off." I was dozing off and on, with my head on Whitey Ford's shoulder, when Casey called out my name. It was the seventh inning of a tied game, and he sent me up to pinch hit. I grabbed a bat, and as I stepped to the plate my head was throbbing and my eyes were blurred. I made up my mind to swing at the first pitch, and I got lucky. The ball landed in the upper deck for a home run, and as I rounded the bases I could see some of the guys in the dugout doubled over with laughter. The fans gave me a standing ovation. As I plopped myself on the bench, I grinned and said to Whitey, "Those people don't know how hard that really was."

They tried to protect Bobby Layne in Pittsburgh and in Detroit, but some nights Bobby just refused to be protected. Once, when he was with the Lions, he had an early morning collision with a parked car. In court his lawyer argued that the slurred speech the arresting officer said he heard was, in fact, just Bobby's Texas accent. He was acquitted.

When Layne walked into the locker room the next day, a sign had been posted that read, AH ALL AIN'T DRUNK, AH'M FROM TEXAS.

His teammates would have killed for him. "When Bobby said block," an end named Buddy Dial once said, "you blocked. When Bobby said drink, you drank."

In Pittsburgh, one of Layne's companions was Ernie Stautner, a defensive tackle with a tough disposition. Stautner was rushed to the hospital one day after a doctor mistakenly injected him with a lethal dosage of a pain medicine. He went into convulsions, and at the hospital the doctors sent for a priest.

Leaning over him, the priest asked if he wanted to confess his sins. Ernie nodded and said, "Yeah, but I don't know how much time I have, Father, so if it's okay with you I'll only hit the highlights." Stautner survived. The tough ones usually do. Sometimes you wish you hadn't left quite so much debris along the way.

There is not a doubt in my mind that in time, my drinking turned us into what is now called a dysfunctional family. I can't spell it, but we were it. My guilt over this was, and is, crushing.

I have had a great life. I was blessed with more natural talent, played for a great team, with great teammates, made a comfortable living for myself and my family, and acquired more fans and friends than anyone could deserve. But the pace I kept made a mess of the lives of my wife and sons. During my years in baseball, I gave myself to the game and all that went with it. Nothing else seemed to matter as much. I loved the game more than I loved myself.

I had a Hall of Fame baseball career, but retired believing I fell short of what I could have achieved, and what my dad had hoped for me and what others expected.

During much of my marriage, I was not a good husband. That was always second to the game. But Merlyn and I never stopped loving each other. We still celebrate our wedding anniversary together, even though we have been separated for the last seven years. My sons looked after their mother, and would see to it if she needed anything. That duty was really mine, but I couldn't face the responsibilities of marriage as my drinking got worse. I did not want to be responsible for anything.

When I was still with the Yankees, I drove a car into a telephone pole and nearly killed Merlyn, whose head struck the windshield. I was drunk and driving too fast.

On another night, Merlyn tried to run me down in the parking lot after I embarrassed her during a dinner with friends. We drank and fought and thought everybody lived like us.

We had four sons. They were all good looking and sweet-tempered. We gave them everything but discipline and a sense of purpose. There was a series of car accidents, tickets for driving while intoxicated, gunplay, two divorces. Billy, our third son, was diagnosed at nineteen with Hodgkin's disease, a form of cancer that attacks the lymph nodes and the bone marrow. He became addicted to painkillers and alcohol. Billy died of a heart attack at thirty-six, a month and a half after I left the Betty Ford clinic. I never felt I was there for him when it mattered.

It's hard to look back. But you learn from it. You hope others can, too. I want to make a difference, not because I hit home runs, but because I changed my life. If I can, anyone can. It is never too late. I have all those letters from people who said that my going public gave them the will or the strength to seek help. Wherever I've gone since leaving rehab, this was the most common reaction.

As nice as it is to hear from strangers that something good has come out of the dumb decisions I made, I wish I could have done this for my sons when they were growing up with a father who was too often absent, or drinking too much.

Even more, I wish I could go back and find that twenty- or twenty-five-year-old Mickey Charles Mantle and talk sense to him, tell him about all the wonders out there waiting for him and about all the mistakes he can avoid if he can only see what is important.

And I would beg him to get it right the first time because you don't get very many second chances. I'm one of the lucky ones who did.

From the time I joined the Yankees in 1951, my view of the world was not much wider than the strike zone. I knew nothing about money and less about being a father, but not many guys did if they grew up in Oklahoma during the years when the Depression and the Dust Bowl met.

My childhood was part of what made me popular with the fans in New York and elsewhere. I was a classic country bumpkin, who came to the big city carrying a cardboard suitcase and with a wardrobe of two pairs of slacks and a pastel-colored sportscoat.

Yet no boy had a more devoted father than Elvin (Mutt) Mantle, and while I may not have been born to play baseball, I only missed it by four years. That was how old I was when my dad started teaching me to switch-hit. He and Grandpa Charlie Mantle both worked in the zinc mines and on weekends pitched in the local semipro leagues.

There were usually three hours of daylight left in the summer when my dad got home, and we spent them playing ball. He pitched to me right-handed and my grandpa pitched to me left-handed, and the two of them taught me to switch-hit before I reached the second grade.

Not that school or anything else mattered much. Mutt Mantle's boy was going to be a big league baseball player, and that was it. The writers never got tired of telling how he named me after Mickey Cochrane, one of his favorites, a catcher who hit .349 for the Philadelphia Athletics the year I was born—1931. I never got tired of it, either.

My father was a quiet man, but he could freeze you with a look. He never told me he loved me. But he showed that he did by all the hours he spent with me, all the hopes he invested in me. He saw his role as pushing me, always keeping my mind on getting better. I worked hard at doing that because I wanted to please him. He would drape an arm around me and give me a hug.

I was the oldest of five kids: the twins, Ray and Roy, my sister, Barbara, and Larry, all four to nine years younger. My mother, Lovell, didn't lavish affection on us either. But she was more vocal and emotional than Dad. Once, when the twins were playing high school football and a fight broke out, she wound up on the field whacking the opposing players on their helmets with her purse.

Mutt Mantle was a chain smoker, as most of the miners were. They didn't see how nicotine could do any more damage to their lungs than the dust they inhaled every day. Dad was a light drinker who bought a half-pint on Saturday and sipped it for days. He would have whipped my fanny if he caught me taking a drink.

Neither of my parents took anything for pain. If my mother had a tooth pulled or gave birth, she wouldn't take so much as an aspirin. I don't know if I inherited their tolerance for pain, or just decided that if you had the right stuff you ignored it.

Mom had been married before, and I had a half-brother and half-sister. She was several years older than my father, but I'm not sure when I knew that. When Mom wanted to show her love she fixed a big meal. For school each day, she handwashed, starched, and ironed my shirt and trousers. She made every baseball uniform I wore up to the time I was sixteen.

Until I signed with the Yankees, I had spent my whole life in a small corner where three states, Oklahoma, Kansas, and Missouri, come together. We moved once to a farm so Grandpa could breathe cleaner air, but we hadn't been there long when he died of Hodgkin's. I was thirteen, and his funeral was the first I ever attended—the first of way too many.

By the time I was fifteen, I was playing town ball against grown-ups and working in the mines with my father. I was as unpolished as the rocks we dug out of the ground, but these were the things that shaped me.

I adored my dad, and was just like him in many ways—I was shy and found it hard to show my emotions. I couldn't open up to people, and they mistook my shyness for rudeness. Of course, sometimes I was just rude. In a way, getting sober opened up a different kind of pain for me. I saw my young life more clearly and I retrieved some memories I would rather have left forgotten. I shared with Merlyn a secret I had kept buried, or concealed, for fifty-odd years.

There is one subject I talked way too much about, and that was my belief that I would die young. I lost my grandfather, my father, and two uncles, all to Hodgkin's disease. None of them lived beyond the age of forty-one. I took it for granted that this would be my fate; it took all the Mantle men. Once I mentioned it for the first time in an interview, it became a part of my permanent record. I'm surprised it didn't turn up on my bubble gum cards.

I don't recall that first interview, but Howard Cosell always took the credit for it. Cosell was good at getting you to tell personal stuff you would rather have kept to yourself. It was strange, though. When I spilled my guts to Howard, almost nobody on the Yankees liked him. Most of the players made him miserable. He was this strange-looking character with a whiny New York accent who prowled our spring training camp trying to get someone to talk to him. This was for radio, and he had a tape recorder with a battery pack that was strapped onto his back. It was the size of a small suitcase.

This must have been the spring of 1956. Of the eighteen seasons I played for the Yankees, I got through a total of three without a serious injury, and that was one of them. I was healthy and had gotten a nice raise and I must have arrived in camp in a good mood, so I gave Cosell an interview. Howard treated me well the rest of my career, but I lost count of the times he used that same angle, "the doomed Yankees slugger, playing out his career in the valley of death."

What I didn't realize was the kind of effect this story would have on my sons. I don't think it sank in that the disease might be passed onto the next generation. But they grew up with the belief that I was going to live to be forty and then die a horrible death. I sure as hell thought so. By the time I turned forty, I couldn't turn off that way of thinking. As my drinking increased, after my separation from Merlyn, I would get paranoid. There were nights when I begged one of the kids not to go out. I had a powerful need to have someone close. I had a terrible fear of getting sick and dying alone.

My greatest regret was that I didn't spend a lot of time with my sons until they became my drinking partners. I just never learned how to be a father.

I remember one Christmas morning when I finished assembling a new bicycle for David, who was going to be eight the next day. He sat on the floor, almost under the tree, and watched with big eyes. I smiled proudly as he rolled it out the door for his first test ride. He climbed on, pushed the pedals—and the bicycle went in reverse.

I looked on, puzzled, but David quickly reassured me: "It's okay, Dad. I can fix it." He picked up the pliers, undid the chains, and put the bike back together. Then he rode off, this time moving forward.

It has been this way most of my life: If I said or did something wrong, the people who might have suffered for it would worry about my feelings being hurt. Even eight-year-olds made excuses for me.

That wasn't the first clue that I wasn't cut out to be a model parent. It became clear to me years ago that I was cut out to be one thing, a baseball player. That is all I was, all I ever wanted to be.

The truth is, I still haven't resolved all the guilt that I feel about my family, and this was a pressure that started after I got sober. I thought I had failed my family in different ways—by not being there for the boys, by not encouraging them more, by not being strict enough. And I felt a huge amount of guilt for having left Merlyn with all of those responsibilities.

We've been married forty-three years, and the first two of those years were unspoiled and perfect. That may sound like one of those stale wedding anniversary gags, but I'm serious. There were other good years, but those two were the last ones before the drinking started. We were both young and unsure and awed by New York, and we clung to each other. Merlyn didn't drink a drop when we were married two days before Christmas 1952. I was just at the two-beers-after-the-game stage. The rules of the road were a little different. If I was invited, I'd have a drink in the hotel bar before bed. This was a kind of starter's kit for new players.

I had jumped from D ball in 1950 to the big leagues in 1951, five classifications, and my life was moving at unbelievable speed. What little I said to the press seemed to amuse them and reinforced the image they were creating—the All-American boy. When I was asked about Merlyn, I told them, "Aw, I've known her since I was a kid in high school." That was just two years earlier.

I was twenty-four when I had my breakout year in 1956, leading the league in hitting (.353), home runs (52), and runs batted in (130). I was the first Yankee to hit more than fifty home runs since Babe Ruth, and the first to win the triple crown since Lou Gehrig in 1934. I also received the Most Valuable Player award.

The next year I won the MVP trophy again, hitting

.365 with 34 homers, even though I reinjured my left leg in September and missed several games. Most of my feelings about falling short in my career go back to those two seasons. A lot of people, including me, thought these should be my typical years, not the peak.

If I had, I might have felt like I deserved to be mentioned with Ruth and Gehrig and DiMaggio. But I tore up my left shoulder in the 1958 World Series against Milwaukee, in a collision with Red Schoendienst, and I was never quite the hitter I had been from the left side of the plate.

I don't like using injuries as an excuse, but I can't deny that I had them, going back to high school. I was kicked in the left shin during football practice and developed chronic osteomyelitis, an inflammation of the bone. The leg was abscessed, swollen to an almost grotesque size and turning purple. I had a fever of 104. But Mom yanked me out of there when a doctor at the first hospital said they might have to amputate. At the next hospital they treated me with a new wonder drug, penicillin, and though I was in bed for weeks and lost thirty pounds, I recovered. I was lucky.

I had regained my speed by the time I signed with the Yankees. Tom Greenwade, who had scouted me, told them about my power, and they were eager to see this kid who hit the ball out of sight from both sides of the plate. But I don't think the reports made it clear how fast I could run. When I went to spring training with the Yankees for the first time, in Phoenix, we ran seventy-five-yard wind sprints and I kept winning all the races. After one of them, I walked off the field and threw up, then I apologized to Casey, explaining that I wasn't yet in shape.

No matter which way the breaks went, I was always lucky. I had been issued a jersey with Number 6 on the back my rookie year—a kind of subtle way of priming the publicity pump. Ruth had worn Number 3, Gehrig was Number 4, and DiMaggio, whose last year was my first, had Number 5.

But when I hit a slump in the middle of my rookie season, and was sent to the minors, Andy Carey, a young third baseman, wound up with Number 6. So when I came back, I inherited the number that became part of my identity—Number 7. I can't even guess at how many photographs showed me swinging from the heels, or kneeling in the on-deck circle, with that blue seven almost jumping off my back. Then there were the photos, too many of them, taken in the locker room of me with a beer can in my hand. I think that is what they call an omen.

There have been three or four versions of some of the events in my life, and I might as well fix this one now. Baseball didn't turn me into a drunk, although I believe now that leaving it speeded up the process.

I drank because I thought we were having fun. It was part of the camaraderie, the male bonding thing. If you were going to be The Man on the field, you had to be The Man off the field. The choice was mine. That was the era, the culture. Fast-buck promoters waved their deals at you, and women waltzed in and out the revolving door. It was a macho time. If you could drink all night, get a girl, get up the next day, and hit a home run, you passed the test.

My drinking increased each year I was with the Yankees, but it wasn't out of control. I didn't need a drink to start my day, and I didn't get drunk every night. I'm not trying to claim that the stories about my barhopping days with Billy Martin and Whitey Ford were exaggerated. Like we said in the TV commercial Whitey and I once made, we probably belonged in the beer drinker's hall of fame. And we put away enough booze to float a battleship.

But with all that, and the injuries, too, I played eighteen years with the Yankees and appeared in more games than any player in the history of the franchise. The Yankees of my time made it to the World Series in twelve of my first fourteen seasons, and I guarantee you nobody will ever match that record.

Billy was gone by the middle of the 1957 season, after the famous party and brawl at the Copacabana. The rest of us partied on. I was young and strong and the ball games gave me a chance to burn off a lot of the toxins.

When my autobiography was published in 1985, I didn't admit I had a problem. I thought back on my playing days and marveled at what an incredible "tolerance" I had for alcohol. But in the last ten years, my system demanded it. I needed a drink early in the day and I needed a bunch of them to finish it, so I could sleep. If I found myself alone in a hotel room with a complimentary bottle of wine from the management, all I had to do was pop the cork. I didn't stop until the bottle was empty.

This may sound as if I am trying to rationalize what I did to myself and to those around me. All I'm trying to do is find my own truth. What I'm really saying is, I drank for just about forty years. My drinking problems grew gradually as each year passed. When I retired in 1969, my drinking became more frequent, and by the 1980s I was a drunk.

In April 1994, I had only recently returned from my treatment for alcohol abuse when I described a drink I called "The Breakfast of Champions" in a *Sports Illustrated* cover story. The ingredients were a shot of brandy, Kahlúa, and heavy cream, tossed into a blender for two minutes and poured over ice in a tall glass. I was trying to come clean about my problem. Calls and letters of support came from everywhere. But there was another side to it. Bartenders started getting orders for it, and I received letters from people wanting to know the exact amounts. I knew many others had serious problems.

I added an epilogue that dealt with my drinking to a book called *All My Octobers,* about my World Series experiences, published that spring.

The fact that I found most amazing was this: I had been a serious drinker for some four decades and the public at large didn't know it. My family, friends, and old teammates knew. Strangers who heard me raising hell in a bar or stumbling through a speech at a banquet knew. But millions of people were unaware that I had a problem until I told them so in January 1994. I did not want any publicity about my stay at the Betty Ford clinic, but the press learned about my seeking help, and it became obvious that the story was going to be printed.

My office in Dallas released a statement admitting that I was suffering from short-term memory loss and blackouts. It didn't mention that my liver was shot and my health was in a steep decline. I thought that if I quit drinking, my blood cell count would rise and my body would begin to heal. My doctors told me I had put my life at risk. But they did not discourage me from believing that the damage could be contained. I believed I could recover my health. Comebacks were not new to me.

I am embarrassed by what I did when I drank: the foul language, the rudeness, having to face people the next day whom I didn't remember insulting the night before. But I am proud that I finally did speak out because I wasn't sure I had the nerve. I almost changed my mind dozens of times. The journey to the Betty Ford Center was long and difficult and tricky, and it began many years ago.

After the 1968 season, I went home to Dallas and began to think about what I would do with the rest of my life. I was worried about having a job and making money. Actually, I have worked at several jobs since my retirement from baseball. I just didn't think of any of these situations as jobs. The money was coming in, more than I made from baseball, but I didn't know if I could count on it. So Merlyn and I sat around and worried, and I tried to get used to not playing baseball for the first time since I was four years old.

I had so many good things happen to me, including the kind of positive attention that few people ever experience. I wish I had enjoyed it more. It was just part of my makeup; I never felt worthy of whatever success I had. I thought I wasted a lot of my talent. This was the way I viewed my life. After I retired from baseball, no matter what I did, I didn't feel natural doing it. Without baseball, I felt I wasn't anybody. My self-worth took a tumble.

Years ago, Roger Kahn wrote an article about the transition I had made from being a "great ballplayer" to being a celebrity. He said I had a status that went beyond the game—I was a folk hero. I never understood that.

Whatever I had become, I had a hell of a time coping with it.

When Gerald Ford was president, the White House invited Merlyn and me to a state dinner honoring the president of France. I couldn't understand what the connection was, why we would belong at a White House dinner. Roy True urged us to go, talked us into it, took care of all the details.

On the day we were to leave, I called Roy at home at five in the morning and told him I had changed my mind and didn't want to go. I didn't know anything about politics and didn't know what to say or how to act. I suspect it took some effort for Roy to keep his voice calm. He said, "Mickey, you don't have a choice now. We have confirmed everything with the White House. We've got a limo set up, hotel rooms, the table and seating arrangements. Merlyn has a beautiful new dress she bought for the occasion. Everything is set. It would be horribly embarrassing for me to call the White House and tell them at the last minute that you have canceled out on them."

Reluctantly, we went. I sat at President Ford's table and we talked about golf most of the night, something we both loved. Merlyn sat with Vice President Nelson Rockefeller, and they talked about each other's children, something they both loved. To our surprise, we had a wonderful time.

We were so elated, and so relieved that it had gone off well, that instead of coming back to Dallas we got on a plane to Las Vegas. I called Roy from there the next day. We had such a fine time, we just didn't want it to end.

There is another story, or myth, that ought to be addressed here. I was never broke, never went bankrupt, and never lacked for a way to make money. But I had an uneasy relationship with high finance. I learned that you have to be careful where and when you lend your name. After a while, I was like the old people who had been through the Depression and kept their money under the mattress.

I was a multimillionaire, on paper, when the company that franchised Mickey Mantle's Country Cookin' went public. A friend told me I should get a lawyer to look at the paperwork, and that was how I met Roy True. A good thing, too. He uncovered fraud in the offering, reported it, and kept me from getting in hot water.

Making money didn't worry me as much as keeping it. At banquets and golf tournaments, I'd hear business people talk about their tax shelters. I thought I paid more than my share of taxes, and that kind of bugged me.

I had a chance to invest in a real estate deal that involved a nice tax write-off. I liked the people and I wanted to take a fourth of it. I asked Roy to check it out, and he said the investment was sound. It amounted to my putting up a little cash and signing a note for $300,000 with the other partners.

Two weeks after we closed the deal, I asked Roy to get me out of it. I couldn't sleep at night. I'd wake up in a cold sweat. I kept thinking about the note I'd signed. Actually, everything was fine, and there was zero chance that I would have to pay it off. But I never could stand the idea of being in debt, of owing anybody. I suppose that trait has to do with how poor I was as a kid, and the way my folks were. We were about the only family in Commerce that didn't buy groceries on credit. We only bought what we needed, and my dad paid cash. The grocer appreciated it so much that he let us kids pick out a free bag of candy.

In 1969, I started to do public appearances. The first one I did was a sports dinner and I gave a speech for $500. Roy taught me how to get on and how to get off. Little by little, I got pretty good at it. But I was still nervous about speaking in public, and I dreaded having to mingle with strangers at the cocktail receptions that always came before the dinner. I'd toss down a couple of vodka and tonics before I made my appearance, and I'd have a couple more during the reception. The appearances were well received, and more requests came in and the price went up. I picked and chose among the events I attended, and no matter how much I drank, I met my commitments.

That first year after I retired, I made more money than I ever had in baseball (the Yankees had paid me $100,000 in each of my last six seasons). Every year, I made more money than I had the year before, but what bothered me was not knowing how to describe what I did for a living. What was I? An endorser? A public speaker? At one point I started to give up my membership at Preston Trail Golf Club, even though playing golf was one of the few interests I still had.

I told a friend, "I just feel bad. Everybody out there has a job. You go in the clubhouse, this guy is an architect, that one is a lawyer. I feel funny. I feel like I don't do anything, like I don't belong."

I kept the membership, and I tried to come to terms with what my line of work was. I was self-employed. I was in public relations. But if I was invited to go on the Johnny Carson show, Roy made sure I was appearing for a particular reason or cause. I wouldn't do one of those celebrity appearances where you just sit on the couch and visit. I didn't want Carson to ask me what I was doing.

Even though I no longer played baseball, I still drank and caroused. That was part of the old life I could take with me. My system needed the jolt that I got from booze. As my body broke down, my ego still needed the company of women.

I didn't realize it, but I was so caught up in the cycle I was in that I missed something big. The country changed. My generation had accepted the idea that it was a fun thing to drink, pick up dates, have a fine time. This was a quality people were thought to admire: He knows how to party. At some point, the mind-set I had known—drinking as a celebration—had almost ceased to exist. The country said, Wait a minute, this is no longer acceptable behavior. I never got that. It blew right by me, and so I didn't make the turn. The way people looked at me out in public, in a restaurant or an airplane or a golf course, changed, too.

I should have seen it coming, because the good and bad times were almost overlapping. In 1970, I came back to the Yankees as a coach under Ralph Houk. I worked with some of the hitters and filled in for Elston Howard as the first base coach during the middle innings, so the fans could see me. They didn't really need me and I felt like a freak. One season was enough.

In January 1974, I was elected to the Hall of Fame, along with Whitey Ford. I was only the seventh player to make it on his first try.

In 1983, I was banned from baseball by the commissioner, Bowie Kuhn, for accepting a job doing sports promotions for the Claridge Hotel and Casino in Atlantic City. He had banned Willie Mays for working at another hotel. At the time, I had no real involvement except for playing in an occasional Old-Timers' Game. He might as well have taken away my TV privileges, but it hurt me and I thought he was wrong for doing that.

Two years later, Willie and I were reinstated by the new commissioner, Peter Ueberroth.

By the late eighties, I was drinking at lunch more frequently. Sometimes that would continue into the night. The weeks, months, and years began to be a blur. I was getting drunk more frequently. My ability to recover from the last hangover was taking two or three days. I developed stomach problems, an ulcer. I was in poor shape and having a harder time hiding it. My doctor friends would stop me on the golf course or in the dining room and urge me to cut back on my drinking.

It was around this time that the memorabilia business just exploded, and my name, my items, my signatures were suddenly very valuable. I started to make more money in a matter of days than I had made in a full season in my prime. There was a boom in the Mickey Mantle industry, but I was drinking more and remembering less.

I started having what came to be called anxiety or panic attacks. I had one flying home to Dallas, after two weeks in Florida for my fantasy camp and two days at a card show in New York. On the plane I began to hyperventilate. I thought I might be having a heart attack, and asked a stewardess if there was a doctor on board. She took one look at me and snapped an oxygen mask over my face. When we landed in Dallas, the paramedics carried me off on a stretcher.

Mickey Jr. was waiting to pick me up, and I'm not sure which of us looked more worried. There was nothing wrong with my heart. The problem was my diet. I was drinking too many of my meals.

In 1987, I met two bright and decent guys who wanted me to put my name on a New York sports bar and restaurant. I became a partner with Bill Liederman and John Lowy, and Mickey Mantle's Restaurant and Sports Bar opened in early 1988 on Central Park South. They did all the work and I made it my New York headquarters whenever I was in town. It's a place where the sports crowd can hang out, like Toots Shor's used to be.

I did make a few suggestions, and I'm proud of one in particular. Not long after we opened, a man with four young kids stopped by my table to ask for autographs. As I was signing, I asked him if everything was all right. He said it was great, and a thrill to meet me, but it was kind of expensive when you have four kids. He said it timidly.

After the family went back to their table, I told the waitress I was picking up their check. Then I waved to Bill and John, and when they came over I asked if we had a menu just for kids. They said we didn't. I told them we needed one. "You've got to take care of the families," I said. Two weeks later, we introduced the Little League menu. My partners say that idea generated more goodwill and more new revenue than any other addition since the restaurant opened.

I was the best man at Billy Martin's wedding. I was a pallbearer at his funeral a year later, after his pickup truck skidded off a snowy road on Christmas Day 1989. There was a question about who was driving, Billy or a friend. There was no question that Billy had been drinking.

When I thought about the great teams I had played on, it was like walking through a cemetery. Cancer killed Roger Maris in 1985. They had buried Casey Stengel ten years earlier. I still remember the first time the Yankees brought me to New York, and the way he cautioned the press to go easy on me. "The kid has never seen concrete," he told them.

I couldn't go on the way I was living, drunk and sick and depressed, covering up with lies, trying to remember where I was going or where I had been. In 1988, I did one of the hardest and dumbest things I ever did—I walked out on Merlyn.

I didn't stop loving her. I just got tired of having to make excuses, having to explain myself. I didn't want to answer to anybody anymore. My behavior was erratic, but leaving was easier than trying to change it.

There was no way I could deal with the guilt I felt at home. I tried not to hurt or embarrass Merlyn in public, but I know I didn't always succeed. I had relationships with many women, two or three that were important to me, that lasted a period of years. In my own way, I cared about them. I revealed myself to them. They knew the good and bad of me. But it wasn't about me falling in love or wanting to marry them. They were not one-night stands. They were not second wives, either. I could never give them my name. I gave that to Merlyn.

And now, I regret this part of my life because of the pain I caused my family. I love my sons dearly and I'm pleased because they are going to be better husbands and fathers than I was. What I did tears my guts out, but I can't undo it.

When Merlyn and I were both drinking she might bring up my affairs and we'd start yelling and cussing. I would never hit her, but Merlyn, tiny as she is, put a lump or two on my head. We would laugh about it, later, sometimes.

There is no way I can put a better spin on this and I won't even try. Merlyn was the only woman I loved for a lifetime, and I didn't want a divorce. She was always going to be my wife, if she wanted to be. I let that be known.

The separation was hard at times, but we talked to each other almost every day, went out to dinner, celebrated our holidays and birthdays and our anniversary. We also shared our losses.

Merlyn was the first member of the family to get into a twelve-step program, which may have been the best thing to come out of our separation. But Danny, our youngest son, was the first one to get into recovery, to actually quit drinking. We didn't get close until he was sixteen, and then we became saloon buddies. When I look back, it was that way with each of the boys. I can't believe what I did to my sons.

For almost two years after Merlyn and I separated, I kept an apartment in Dallas and spent much of my time at my apartment at the Regency Hotel in New York. Then I built a house in Dallas and lived there with Danny and his soon-to-be wife, Kay Kollars, after that.

In September 1993, Danny flew with me to Los Angeles, where I was doing an autograph signing for Upper Deck. He met a friend who lived out there, and instead of helping me with the signings, he took off. They went on a bender, but instead of going back to Dallas he checked himself into the Betty Ford Center. I had no idea where he was. When I found out, my feelings were really jumbled. I was angry and felt betrayed. I told people I thought he shouldn't have spent his money on a problem that wasn't that bad.

How could I not notice that he needed help? I guess I was too busy pretending that I didn't. During 1993, depression was a regular part of my life. At times, I thought about killing myself.

Kay joined him a few days later and went through the program herself. When they returned to Dallas, I asked them a lot of questions. I was nibbling at it, trying to imagine what kind of place it was, and how humiliating it might be. Merlyn took her last drink the day she left Palm Springs, after visiting Danny during family week. I didn't go. I wish I had.

Things started to come together to force my decision. In December, at a charity golf tournament near Atlanta, I made a complete fool of myself. I had been drinking all day and I was cursing and crude before the dinner even started. Then during the course of the evening I referred to Reverend Wayne Monroe, who was in charge of the charity, by saying, "Here's the fucking preacher."

As soon as I got back to Dallas, I started asking Danny and Kay more questions. I had lunch with Danny and Pat Summerall, who played football for the New York Giants and went on to a long career as a broadcaster. Pat was a friend of mine who had gone to the Betty Ford Center and gotten sober. I asked them both, Do you have to get up and talk in front of strangers? Do they lay a lot of religion on you?

The answers were, Yes, you have to share your story with strangers. No, the chapel is there if you want it, but they don't put a God trip on you. I've always prayed, but when I was little my folks didn't believe you had to go to church to have faith. I'm sort of the same way. I don't think religion ought to be a spectator sport.

I had my doctor give me a complete head-to-toe physical, and I spent an hour and fifteen minutes in an MRI tube getting my liver examined. The next day, after he studied the results, the doctor laid it out for me: "Mickey, your liver is still working, but it has healed itself so many times that before long, you're just going to have one big scab there. Eventually you'll need a new liver. Look, I'm not going to lie to you. The next drink you take might be your last."

I asked Roy True to have someone make the reservations for me to fly to Palm Springs and check into the Betty Ford Center. Everyone around me sort of held their breath, waiting to see if I would go through with it. I wasn't sure myself. It was touch and go. I knew I needed help, but I worried about spilling my guts in front of people I didn't know. Hell, I couldn't do it with people who had known me all their lives.

The key was whether I got on the airplane. My friends know that once I start something, I don't quit. So I got on the plane and I flew to Palm Springs and I spent thirty-two extraordinary days getting the help that might have kept me from killing myself. This time I wasn't Mickey Mantle. I was just the guy in Room 202. One of the first things you have to do is open up to the members of your dormitory in group therapy sessions. It took me a couple of times before I could talk without crying.

You're supposed to say why you're there, and I said I had a bad liver and was depressed. Whenever I tried to talk about my family, I got all choked up. I had to talk about how I had screwed up my kids by not being a real father. I said that Mickey Jr. could have been a major league baseball player if my dad had been his dad. I've never heard my sons blame me for not being there. But they don't have to . . . I blame myself.

The program at Betty Ford is based on the twelve steps of Alcoholics Anonymous. When you go through the first step, you have to tell your life story to your group. They ask you to tell stories of the things you did when you were drunk, how it made you feel, and the things that really bothered you later.

The most important breakthrough I had at Betty Ford happened in grief therapy groups. During my preadmission interview, I told the counselor that I drank because of depression. I had to write my father a letter and tell him how I felt about him. You talk about sad. It only took me ten minutes to write the letter and I cried the whole time, but after it was over I felt better. I said I missed him, and I wish he could have lived to see that I did a lot better after my rookie season with the Yankees. I told him I had four boys—he died before my first son, Mickey Jr., was born— and I told him that I loved him. I wish I could have told him that when he was still alive.

The more I came to grips with my feelings, the worse I felt about how I had neglected my family. I felt so guilty and didn't want to face them at family week during my stay. Instead, I had my current girlfriend come to visit. It just seemed safer than having to face my family. I always felt bad that I did that.

You have to keep a journal and put down the word or words that express your feelings. I brought that home with me. In the margins, on all four pages, the words are *embarrassed, angry with myself, angry, humiliated, foolish, ashamed, stupid, guilty, inadequate, exasperated.* In the dictionary of self-loathing, I don't think I missed much. But it helped me face my faults and my mistakes. I felt different and I was determined to stay sober.

You had to list examples of your chemical abuse and your loss of control. I mentioned how, when I learned I had a diseased liver, I switched from hard stuff to wine and thought I was helping myself. I wrote down how, a year before, I woke up in Merlyn's house and had no idea where I was or who I was with.

I lost ten pounds and felt better than I had in years. I called Pat Summerall and told him, "If you ever see me start to take a drink, I want you to promise to put a bullet in my head."

Sober, I finished my stay and came home. I soon got a terrible and painful test of my recovery.

In March, just weeks after I came out of Betty Ford, our son Billy died of a heart attack at thirty-six. But it started with Hodgkin's. For seventeen years, Billy went through a cycle of being ill, enduring chemotherapy, being in remission, getting hooked on prescription drugs and alcohol, and finally wearing out his heart.

I have never felt so helpless as I did watching Billy suffer at his young age. He spent a year in Houston taking an experimental chemotherapy treatment, and it amounted to a brutal attack on his body. The first night or two, his screams kept the entire floor awake. Then, and for years to come, Merlyn took care of Billy and dealt daily with his problems.

I wish it had been me. I wish I could have taken the cancer from him. He was in drug and alcohol treatment four times in four years. In 1993, he had heart bypass surgery and two valves were replaced. Merlyn had heart surgery the same week.

Danny brought the news of Billy's death to me in the locker room at Preston Trail. I saw the tears running down his face and I knew. Now I had to tell Merlyn that Billy was dead. After all we had been through, this was the most agonizing thing I've ever had to do.

She had taken him to halfway houses, bailed him out of jail for DWI, cared for him at home. A large part of her life for the past several years had been Billy. She collapsed in my arms.

I could not help but think, and still think, that if I had stopped drinking earlier, if I had cleaned up my act, I might have been able to help Billy. I might have kept him off the drugs. His heart might not have been so weakened.

There is a great closeness and tenderness among the boys that pleases me mightily—Mickey Jr., now forty-two; David, thirty-nine; and Danny, thirty-five [their ages in 1995]. A month after we buried Billy, Danny and Kay were married. A year later, my mother died at the age of ninety-two. She was in a nursing home in Joplin, Missouri, just over the state line from Commerce, a nice place with good care, and Danny and I drove over to see her shortly before her death. I was glad we could do it when we were both sober.

I had been to two funerals and a wedding in a span of

about seven months, and I knew I was going to stay sober. If Billy's death didn't tempt me to drink, nothing would. I had one close encounter. I was at the club, alone, and the bar was empty. I thought, Well, I could probably have one quick drink, maybe a glass of wine, and what would be the harm?

Then I reached in my pocket for my car keys and headed to the parking lot. Not this time.

David was the next Mantle to go through Betty Ford, and he wound up writing a letter to me. Mickey Jr. is the last now, and we are all encouraging him. He's hardheaded, like me, and he won't give you his word until he is certain he will keep it.

Our lives have been in shambles for a lot of years, much of it flowing from my drinking. But I think it is going to turn out all right. We have drawn closer and we're able to be more open about expressing our feelings. I love my family and they love me. I just have to learn to love myself.

Mantle was taken by ambulance to the Baylor University Medical Center on May 28, 1995. He had been suffering from stomach cramps for weeks and could no longer ignore them. The diagnosis was liver cancer. He underwent an organ transplant on June 8, and doctors declared the surgery a success, but warned of the danger of recurrence. He was to be placed on a form of chemotherapy to guard against it. He was discharged one month after he had been admitted. He said he was feeling better than he had for many years.

He held a cheerful news conference at the hospital on July 11, during which he noted he had lost forty pounds.

With a thumb, gesturing at himself, he said, "This is a role model. Don't be like me."

On July 28, Mantle taped a statement disclosing that cancer had spread to his new liver, lungs, and pancreas. He thanked the fans for their get-well wishes and prayers, and urged them to support the organ donor program. Over the next ten days, he had one chemotherapy treatment and two blood transfusions. His doctors said he had a cancer that was "the most aggressive anyone on the medical team had seen."

Mickey Charles Mantle died at 1:10 A.M. on August 13, 1995. He was sixty-three. His wife, Merlyn, and his son David were at his bedside, each holding one of his hands.

Prior to his death, Mickey kept a vow to form the Mickey Mantle Foundation and dedicated much of the last weeks of his life to reviewing and approving the plans and mission of the foundation.

Mickey Jr. entered the Betty Ford clinic in October 1995, and completed his stay in mid-November. He is alcohol- and drug-free and continues his recovery every day, one day at a time.

Part Two

Merlyn

I didn't know how to dress or how to wear makeup or how to ask for advice. Neither did Mick, who owned one pair of shoes and a big, wide tie with birds on it when he first came to New York.

Chapter 2

Young Love

NOT EVERYONE CAN PICK OUT A CERTAIN DAY, DECADES later, and say, That was when my life changed forever. I can. The date was October 6, 1949.

The crowd began filling up the small stadium early that night. It was the night of the big game between Picher and Commerce high schools, the hot rivals in that part of Oklahoma.

I was on the sidelines with the band and my best friend, another majorette named Lavanda Whipkey. We were looking up at the stands, checking out the early arrivals—in small towns you know everybody. We noticed these two good-looking guys, one blond with a crewcut, the other dark-haired, both wearing Commerce football jackets.

Of course, we zeroed in on them real fast. Lavanda happened to know the blond one. "Oh, there's Mickey

Mantle," she said, nodding in his direction. She said he had just returned home from his first season of playing ball for a New York Yankees farm team.

The name was unknown to me, and I didn't recall ever seeing him play. The star athlete at Commerce was Bill Moseley. Everyone knew Bill.

But that night Lavanda and I had our eye on these two guys in the letter jackets. My sister, Pat, was dating someone from Commerce—we lived in Picher—and we asked her to introduce us. They asked us for a date that Saturday night, and I wound up with the dark-haired one. Lavanda was with Mickey.

With some of his bonus money, Mickey had bought a fancy two-toned 1947 Chevrolet Fleetline with mohair seats and a vacuum shift. On the basis of that car alone, he would have qualified as a man about town, except for the fact that he was so shy he hardly spoke a word.

Later, Mick told me it was the first decent car his family ever owned. For years his dad drove an old, beat-up La Salle, and he would take the back seat out of the car so he could carry livestock in it. If he bought a calf at sale, he would just put it in the space where the back seat had been.

Mick learned to drive on that old La Salle. But now he had this flashy Chevy Fleetline, and we all piled in and drove to a place called the Spook Light, a deserted spot near the town of Seneca. It was a popular parking spot for young couples, and the source of several legends.

If you waited long enough, at certain, unpredictable times a ghostly light could be observed through the trees. There were tales of murders and headless Indians and haunted lovers. But the waiting was the best part. Mostly, the kids went there to smooch. We also called it necking, and it was just what the word implied, a very limited form of romance.

A couple of nights later, Mick called Lavanda for another date and it turned out she was busy. So he decided to try me next. He called and asked me out and I said yes.

A date was a movie, followed by a stop at the local drive-in. Mick had a hamburger and a hot chocolate. I just had the hot chocolate because I was too shy to eat in front of him. We just hit it off and dated steadily all through my senior year.

We were younger than the eighteen- or nineteen-year-olds are today. In the fifties, a date could be a long walk. I developed an instant crush on Mickey Mantle, and by our second or third date, I was in love with him and always would be.

Growing up, I spent a lot of hours daydreaming. I was starstruck. I loved movies, Hollywood, that whole fantasy world. When I was in grade school, you could mail twenty-five cents to the movie studios and get a signed photo of your favorite stars. I was a fan of Lana Turner, Ava Gardner, and Gene Tierney. I spent one of my quarters on a picture of Guy Madison, who starred in a few westerns, but never made it big.

I had some talent, and a certain local recognition, as a singer. I started taking voice lessons when I was twelve, and that was what I hoped would be my future. My senior year in high school, I won a scholarship to Miami (Oklahoma) Junior College. In my dream world, I wanted to be in show business and live in California. But I didn't let my mind run wild, thinking about a career on the radio, or cutting records, or singing with a small, respectable band. At least, I figured, I could make a living as a music teacher.

I sang at school, at church, and once at Camp Crowder, as part of a group that entertained the troops during the war. I even won a music contest, singing an aria in Italian. I don't know how I learned the words, but I did. I was shy and unsure of myself in so many other ways, but I enjoyed the singing and even the crowds. This was the one place I could open up. The band leader at school was also my voice teacher, Mrs. Ireba Edwards, and she often accompanied me on the piano. She pushed me and encouraged me.

But once Mickey Mantle came into my life, I forgot about anything else: junior college, singing, show business, and California. They just sort of vanished from my mind, and I can't say that I ever dwelled on them, or had any great regrets.

I had a boyfriend when I met Mick, and it strikes me as funny now when I think about the nervous week I spent rearranging my datebook. What attracted me to the other boy was mainly the fact that he owned a motorcycle. I loved motorcycles, a weakness I may have passed on to my son David.

Once, in what passed for semishameless behavior in those days, I had an early date with my biker and a late date—for a football game—with Mickey. I was on the back of the motorcycle, going home after a movie, when we passed Mick on the side of the road, fixing a flat tire on his car. He had his head down, getting the tire on, and didn't see me. I made myself very small. I had to move fast to get rid of my other date before Mick showed up. But the way my heart was pounding, I knew I didn't want to see anyone else, not from then on.

I just fell hard for Mick. He was as shy as I was, maybe more, and I liked that about him. His shirts were always starched, and I liked the scent of his aftershave lotion. He always smelled good, and he had a fresh and outdoorsy look. Mick was nineteen, a year older than me, and we never touched a drop of alcohol on our dates.

But even then, I've learned from my recovery, I had some of the tendencies of a problem drinker. I didn't like to be in a crowd. I went into a shell around strangers. I was quiet and sometimes withdrawn. I was the type that could be lonely in a room filled with 500 people. This wasn't a good omen for Mick or me, but it would be a long while before we knew about such things.

I was brought up in a religious home. My grandfather was a deacon in the Baptist church. My father was a deacon and a member of the school board. Both our parents came from good Midwestern stock. The Johnsons were Scandinavian, and I'm told that is a race that enjoys its spirits. I believe there was alcoholism in my dad's family, but nobody talked about it.

Those were simple times and simple pleasures. But I was a restless girl who couldn't identify her longings. I worried about leading a life of boredom and tedium. An exciting night for me was to stay over at a girlfriend's house. On Saturday night, payday at the mines, people drove into town to do their shopping. My sister and I would drop by the drugstore to have a milkshake or a malt, and watch the men stagger out of the bars across the street. Drinking in our small community was considered something sinful. Nobody thought of it as an illness.

Our parents were wonderful, loving and kind and

interested in their daughters. They came to school functions. They took us on trips.

We were considered well off by the standards of that time and place, the Oklahoma of the *Grapes of Wrath* era. Working in the lead and zinc mines was hard and dangerous and the men made almost nothing. My grandfather went into the lumber business, and did well enough to sponsor a team in the summer leagues. Mick told me he used to hear the references to the Johnson Lumber Company on the megaphone at the ballpark. He teased me about it, saying he thought we had lots of money.

On both sides of our family, our grandparents had trades or businesses and they lived in nice homes.

An early trauma in my life came when my dad worked in the mines and suffered a head injury. He had to undergo surgery to remove a blood clot, and this left him an epileptic. We lived with the fear of his having a seizure. He could, and did, have them just driving his car, or in his sleep. He never went back to the mines, and worked in the office at the lumber yard.

My folks loved Mick, the childlike sweetness of him, and my mother does to this day. Even after we separated, he was always nice to her. Every Christmas he sent her a check. She looked forward to that, living on a small income.

The Mantles were respected in town as good, hardworking people. They were a family of athletes, including the cousins, and all over the area Mick was looked at as a kind of flag-bearer, headed for the big time. He always said his father, Mutt, would have been a big leaguer if he had been given the chance Mick had. His granddad, too.

The feeling between Mutt Mantle and his son was

more than love. Mick was his work of art, just as much as if his father had created him out of clay. He spent every minute he could with him, coaching, teaching, shaping him, pointing him toward the destiny he knew was out there. Baseball consumed Mickey. He talked, when he talked, of little else. It was the number one priority in his life and, in a way, always would be.

Mrs. Mantle, Lovell (the emphasis on -*vell*), was not a warm or openly affectionate woman, but she was a tireless and protective mother. She had seven children, two by a first marriage, and I never saw anyone do as much laundry. She did it by hand, on a washboard in the back yard, and hung it on row after row of clotheslines to dry. They lived in the country and didn't yet have electricity.

Mick's parents were a typical couple for those times. She was twenty-seven, ten years older than Mutt when they married. Little was known about her first marriage. Her daughter, Anna Bea, married young, left home, worked as a barmaid, and died in her twenties. Hers was a short, sad life.

Mick's half-brother, Theodore, was a hard drinker. He didn't have the money to be classy with his drinking, but he was a generous person who would give away what little he had. When he was discharged from the army, he gave Mick most of his mustering-out pay to buy my wedding ring.

We went together for two years before we married. We went steady for one year and were engaged for another. Once Mick left for the rookie camp in Phoenix, at the end of January 1950, about the only contact we had for the next six months was through the mail.

We wrote nearly every day. This was still a time when long distance phone calls were considered a luxury. They were mainly reserved for emergencies: a loved one was sick, or had a baby, or someone needed money, or you were homesick to the point of being desperate.

In our part of Oklahoma, we still had crank telephones at home. You would give the handle a couple of spins, the operator came on the line, and you gave her the number to dial. You took it for granted that she would listen in on the conversation. The telephone operator knew all the gossip in town: which couples were dating, which ones were breaking up.

A year later, when I joined Mickey in New York, I was half afraid to make a call because I had never used a rotary phone before. Looking back, we were pretty backwoodsy, certainly compared to New York.

The innocence, warmth, and sweetness of Mick came through in the letters he wrote, the first ones from the Yankees minor league camp in Phoenix. Nearly all of his letters began the same way—"Dearest Merlyn, Hi, hon . . ."—so I won't keep repeating the terms of endearment.

They were addressed to Miss Merlyn Johnson, Picher, Oklahoma, and that was all the information the post office needed.

January 23, 1950

. . . You have heard of Jackie Jensen, from California, the All-American? Well, he's out here. There is about five New York Yankees out here. I am in a cabin with three other boys. Two of them played on our team with Joplin last year.

Boy, it sure is pretty out here. This place we're staying at is alright. There is a swimming pool right behind our cabin.

How is your Mother and Dad and Pat? Tell them all I said hello. Sure do wish you were out here. We could really have a swell time. I just found out that we are going to the DOG RACES tonight . . .

All My Love, Mick

A few days later, he complained about my letters being on the skimpy side.

January 28, 1950

I just received your very short letter. I just got set down to read it when I was through with it. But I sure was glad to hear from you. All we do is play baseball all day from 8 A.M. to 3:30 P.M. I sure miss you a lot. I tell the boys here how good looking you are and everything and they say no one is that good.

If you have any little snapshots of you send them down here to me, will you? How did the Commerce Junior High come out in the tournament?

We have been to town twice since we've been here and it's just about as dead as Picher. Not quite, though. This is the craziest climate I ever saw. You smother in the day and freeze at night.

Love, Mick

February 9, 1950

Just got back from the ball park and got your letter. I feel a lot better now . . .

Honey, I don't believe I will ever want to break up with you. You haven't been doing anything to cause us to break up, have you?

. . . You probably won't understand the clipping about the home runs and triple. You can have your dad explain it to you.

March 8, 1950
Lake Wales, Fla.

I guess right about now you are over at Miami Teen-Town, while I am sitting up here in this old hotel thinking about you.

There's a little beer joint right across the street from the hotel, where you can buy beer for ten cents a glass. All they have on the juke box is hill billy music. You know, the kind you like. Won't but one guy go over there with me. The rest are afraid of getting caught in there.

There are two guys rooming with me. Right next door to us is a newlywed couple. They really give that old bed hell. Well, I had better close for now. I love you . . .

March 24, 1950

Boy, you should see me. Yesterday me and Dave Waters laid out in the sun and I really am sunburnt. On top of that, I got a G.I. haircut.

I was talking to Lee McPhail [sic], the guy who tells you where we are going to play, and he said I could go to Joplin [MacPhail was then the Yankees' farm director, later their general manager, and eventually the president of the American League].

You say you will probably not be lucky enough to

have me for always. Well, honey, I'll let you in on a little secret. I'm yours for as long as you want me. If you could see me now, it probably wouldn't be for very long . . .

His next few letters kept me up to date on his sunburn. It was bad enough to keep him out of two games. I could just picture him: His face was bright pink, his nose peeling, his back blistered. His skin was so fair, he would get sick from too much sun.

March 23, 1950

We had a shuffleboard tournament in the lobby last night. Each man gives a quarter to enter. Then they put everyone's number in a cap and draw for partners. Me and Jim Ludtke won it. We got three dollars apiece.

. . . The other night I went to the movie show and saw "They Live by Night." There was a girl in it that reminded me of you.

Everyone down here seems to be married, but only a few bring their wives. If you and I ever get married, you are going everywhere this boy goes. I wish you were here now . . .

That year, 1950, Mickey and his dad used to come by and get me when the team was at home, and I rode with them to the ballpark in Joplin. We always laughed about the way Mick's dad drove. He never went over thirty miles an hour. He would pick me up so early we would be the only ones in the park, except for the players. I hated the waiting, but that was Mr. Mantle's favorite time of the day. He liked to watch the players straggle onto the field at practice. He loved to listen to the sports news on the car radio and the announcements over the public address system at the ballpark.

The PA system was an old man with a deep voice and a megaphone.

But I got to know Mick's family well. They were all nuts about sports—the twins, Roy and Ray, the youngest brother, Butch, his sister, Barbara. His mom always kept a scorecard at the game. Mick's dad never sat with her. She would get so involved, she embarrassed him, yelling at the umpires and shouting advice to the players. So he always sat by himself.

When I graduated from high school that spring, Mick drove me to Joplin to pick out two new dresses. His salary then was $250 a month, but he took me to Kassab's, the nicest store in town. I was so happy, so proud of my graduation gift, I might as well have been shopping in New York.

Mick made a lot of errors at shortstop that year, fifty or so. But he was getting to be real popular with the fans, especially the young female ones. For the first time in my life I knew how it felt to be insanely jealous. If I saw the girls kind of fawning over him, I would always have something to say about it. He thought it was funny, my getting upset that way.

By the end of the season, Mickey had been called up from Joplin in mid-September to join the Yankees in time for their final road swing. He was just along for the ride, but I saved his first "big league" letter.

September 18, 1950
St. Louis, Mo.

I just got back from the ball park. The Yankees won one and lost one today. We leave for Chicago tonite.

There were 21,000 people at the game just to see *me* and guess what? I didn't get to play . . . I told Casey that if I didn't get to play I was going home, so I expect to be in the lineup tomorrow. (Ha, ha.)

He never did get into a game in those final two weeks, but he hadn't expected that he would. By the time he returned to Commerce, I had graduated and taken a job at the First State Bank of Picher. I wasn't trying to pry, but I always knew how much money Mickey and his dad made because their paychecks came through our bank.

That was the last winter, 1950, that Mick worked with his dad in the mines. Payday was Saturday and they cashed their checks at the Safeway store, when his dad bought their groceries. Mutt Mantle made about a hundred dollars a week, which in the fifties was very good money. Of course, he had a houseful of kids to feed and clothe. There was just my sister and me in our family, so we didn't have nearly the obligations Mick's parents had.

In the farming and mining towns, most people worked six and seven days a week. It was commonplace to cash a paycheck at the grocery store, where you could buy food on credit and take care of the bill on payday.

I was still restless, eager to see what was beyond the state line. I wanted a different life, and Mick made that available to me. He was making news, going places, and that was exciting to me. I didn't need a life of my own. I could get involved in his. I was already proud of him. He was a year or two ahead of schedule, but the big leagues were his next stop.

We saw each other nearly every day that winter and

then, suddenly, it was spring and he was back in Phoenix, this time training with the Yankees—and, to borrow a phrase from the sports page, burning up the Cactus League.

His letters had a whole new intensity now.

March 21, 1951

How are you getting along at the bank?

... When I start writing a letter, I always say to myself—"I won't tell her I love her until about the middle of the letter." But after I finish and read it over it is all the way through it.

Honey, yesterday about nine of us went to the MGM studios. We met a whole bunch of movie stars, including Spencer Tracy, Gene Kelley [sic], Jane Greer, Betty Grable, Debbie Reynolds, Jean Peters, Gloria De Haven, Clifton Webb, Arlene Dahl, Red Skelton, Esther Williams and Howard Keel. Out of all the girls I saw, there wasn't any as pretty as you . . .

Mick went north with the Yankees to open the season, and started in right field, with Joe DiMaggio in center and Gene Woodling in left. He had an early season crisis, but that was the year he fulfilled his father's lifelong dream.

The Mantles never lived in a modern home, with indoor plumbing, until Mickey had his first success with the Yankees and bought them one. When they lived in the country, his mother heated water on the stove every morning for him to bathe in. All of his clothes were starched and when he left for school he was scrubbed and clean, immaculately so.

And yet the early pressure on Mickey to play ball, and his self-imposed drive to play it better than anyone, caused real emotional problems for him. A lot of the conflicts in him later had their roots in those years. Mick wet his bed until he was sixteen years old.

I would hope that this would not be taken as demeaning him. But it is important, I think, in understanding what he went through, and how much he wanted to please his dad. This is what the pressure of wanting that approval did to him. He told me that he knew from the time he was five years old that he wanted to be a ballplayer, and how he could never face his father if he didn't make it to the major leagues.

Interestingly, the bed-wetting stopped when the Yankees sent him to Independence, Missouri, for his first season in Class D. He had to solve the problems before any of his teammates found out. He could not abide anyone making fun of him. He stopped by asserting his own pure willpower, because the pressure didn't end then, or with the Yankees. It never ended.

I know exactly how much he ached for his dad's approval. His sons and I felt the same way about Mick. And until late in his life, until he got sober, he couldn't give us much. If he finished dinner and said, "That was good," my heart leaped like a fawn. It was hard for him to give compliments. He received them all his life and did not handle those well. He seldom thought he deserved them.

You could write a whole book on his relationship with his father, who had this wonderful but obsessive dream for Mickey, and only for Mickey. He was anointed from the cradle. When his dad would pitch to him for hours, out of a hundred pitches, Mick would be in terror of missing one and looking bad, and having his father frown or criticize him.

I was with the two of them in the Aladdin Hotel in Kansas City in 1951, after the Yankees had sent Mickey back to the minors. They were hoping he could regain his confidence and his batting stroke. He had struggled in New York, and they couldn't afford to play him in the heat of a pennant race.

Mickey was like a whipped pup in Kansas City, and things hadn't improved for him. He told Mutt on the phone that he didn't think he could make it, he wasn't hitting at this level, either. His father picked me up and we made the five-hour drive from Commerce. That day he was clearly looking for sympathy, and maybe the message that if he failed it wouldn't be the end of the world. But Mutt swung his suitcase out of the closet and started throwing his clothes into it. "I thought I raised my son to be a man," he said, "not a quitter. Well, I was wrong. You can come back and work in the mines with me."

Mick had to plead with him before he convinced him that he knew now that he was wrong. He had been moping around feeling sorry for himself. He was going to change his attitude. He was going to be okay. And Mutt calmed down. He even smiled.

After that, Mickey went on a hitting spree. By now I knew what a run batted in was, and Mick had something like fifty of them in forty games. The Yankees called him up from Kansas City at the end of August.

From the start of the season, he had written me short, sweet letters filled with wonder. He told me he loved me and missed me. He wrote me about moving in with two veterans, Johnny Hopp and Hank Bauer, and how they lived above a deli. He would run down and pick up their orders for lunch or dinner. He said he tried something called "matzoh ball soup," and really liked it.

Once he wrote, "I think the fans are really beginning to like me. I hit a homer yesterday to win a game, and they stood up and cheered. Later, I posed for a picture with a well known black boxer." I used to wonder who the boxer was, and what became of him, but Mick didn't know.

That fall, he started in right field in the World Series against the New York Giants, playing next to DiMaggio. It was in Game 2 that he broke his right kneecap chasing a fly ball off the bat of Willie Mays. While DiMaggio was making the catch, Mickey's spikes caught on a sprinkler head. He wound up in the hospital and, ironically, his father shared the room with him. They were holding onto each other's shoulders, and Mutt sort of caved in as they got out of the cab. One doctor repaired Mickey's knee, and another broke his heart. He told him his father was dying of Hodgkin's disease and to take him home. There was nothing anyone could do for him.

Mick had been dating a New York showgirl, and he introduced her to his father. She also had hooked up with an agent who arranged for her to have fifty percent of Mickey's contract for life. There was a side of him that would always be drawn to that kind of woman.

In those days, Mickey believed nearly everything he heard and trusted just about anyone he met.

Somehow, the Yankees got him out of the clutches of the agent he had signed with, and then Frank Scott, who represented several of the Yankees and was well respected, took Mickey on as a client.

I knew none of this until months or years later, including what Mick's father told him he wanted for Christmas, after they learned that Mutt was dying. His dad told him that he wanted Mick to marry me; that was the best present he could give him—and, in time, a freckle-faced, redheaded grandson. He told Mick, "You'll be happy with Merlyn. She's your kind." Meaning, we were raised alike, from the same soil.

That explained the timing when Mickey asked me to marry him. We had been engaged for most of 1951 and now it was the middle of November. He picked me up for one of our movie dates, and on the way he said, "Do you want to get married?"

I was startled. I said, "Well, yes." It was all I had really wanted since the second or third time I had seen him.

He said, "Then why don't we do it about Christmas-time?"

I wasn't aware then that he was fulfilling his father's wish. But I knew his father liked me and thought we were good together.

The wedding was small, which was a fortunate thing because we were married in my parents' home, and it had only four rooms. Just our immediate families attended. My mother's cousin played the wedding march on the piano, and the minister from our church performed the ceremony. On December 23, 1951, I became Mrs. Mickey Mantle.

The wedding was happy and tearful at the same time. His father looked on, and we both knew this ceremony was partly for him. Next to me, the groom's father was the happiest person in the room. Mick was somewhere in the top five. He would have done anything for his parents, and his lingering sadness was the fact that he was not able to do it sooner.

It was a busy winter. With his World Series check, he made the down payment on a seven-room house for his parents in Commerce. The cast on his leg was removed in mid-November. And we were married two days before Christmas.

I knew that we loved each other. I also knew that marriage was not a real high priority for Mick—he was twenty years old and just starting to live his dream. He didn't plan it. He didn't have to, it was just the way he was. He was married, but in a very small geographic area of his mind.

He treated marriage as he did most things, a sort of party with added attractions. Bill Moseley and his wife went with us on our honeymoon. It was one of those Mickey Mantle production numbers, where someone had promised him a free weekend in Hot Springs, Arkansas, and the bridal suite at a plush hotel. Hot Springs was a lively town, with gambling and fancy clubs where great entertainers like Sophie Tucker and Bing Crosby would perform.

Unfortunately, when we arrived no one had ever heard of our host, and there were no reservations and no free weekend. We rented our rooms for one night. The next morning, we had breakfast and then drove back to Commerce to begin our married life. We moved into a small motel on Main Street, called Dan's Motor Court. It had open draft heaters, and Mickey's dad would stop by every night to see that we were okay. He was afraid that the fire might go out, and gas would leak from the heater and we would die in our sleep. It was typical of him, but we thought he was worrying needlessly.

I probably still thought so until I heard a couple of years ago about Vitas Gerulaitis, the tennis player, dying from gas fumes in a friend's cottage.

It was just a cheap motel, but it fit our budget. Recently, going through some of our papers, I found Mick's contract for the 1952 season. It was for the same salary he had made the year before, $7,500, with an incentive clause that paid him another $2,500 if he was still with the team in June. I don't know if the Yankees wanted to keep him hungry and insecure, or if they had doubts about how well his knee would hold up.

But it was fortunate that Mickey had an off-season job with a man we both came to love, Harold Youngman. He paid Mick $300 a month to make some trips for his construction company in Baxter Springs. Harold wanted him to learn the business, but he also liked to show him off to his customers. Harold and his wife, Stella, looked on us as the kids they never had.

Most of the players needed second jobs, unless they were stars or had been in the league a long while. I didn't know much about baseball, but I knew instinctively that no matter what Mickey was paid, we would be living beyond our means.

He had not made an effort to rehabilitate his knee, and he was still limping when he left for spring training. So there was some uncertainty about the season. The good news was that I went with him. The Yankees trained in St. Petersburg, and it was my first trip to Florida. It was just about my first trip to anywhere that was more than five hundred miles from home.

In the fifties, and for some years after, St. Petersburg was the kind of town where people would go to visit their parents. You would see a lot of shuffleboard courts at all the hotels. But the baseball teams enlivened things considerably, and it was a lovely, romantic spring. We found an apartment on the beach, with a picture window that gave us a sweeping view of the ocean.

Then the team broke camp and headed north to open the season. As exciting as it was to see New York and to be a part of it, I got an early taste of what a rollercoaster ride was in store for us, this and any baseball season.

Mickey still wasn't ready to play every day. And in contrast to the clean air and swaying palms and sandy beaches of Florida, we had a tiny, bleak room at the Concourse Plaza Hotel. We had a bed, a chair, one closet, and a bathroom. There was no stove or refrigerator and we couldn't afford to rent a television set, at ten dollars a month. Mickey needed to send money home to help his family. His father was at a clinic in Denver, alone. He didn't want his children to see him sick and dying. This was how he wanted it.

When the team left to go on a road trip, the wives would get together, take turns and cook. That part was fun, and you tried to tune out the occasional cutting remarks. If two husbands both played, say, left field, there was sometimes more rivalry between the wives than the men.

I felt shy and out of place, as I often did, but New York magnified these feelings. I didn't know how to dress or how to wear makeup or how to ask for advice. Neither did

Mick, who owned one pair of shoes and a big, wide tie with birds on it someone gave him when he first came to New York. In time, we learned to ask. In those early days, as I walked around, it seemed to me that most of the women in New York were beautiful and smartly dressed. But I was careful not to drop my complaints, or my doubts, on Mick. He had all he could handle.

On May 6, 1952, Casey Stengel reached Mickey in our room and gave him the message he had been dreading. His mother had called Yankee Stadium and left word that his father was dead. He was thirty-nine years old.

Everything about that day is still vivid to me. Mickey pounded his fist against the wall. And then he asked me to leave the room. I was stunned. I walked to the door and said, "When are we going home?"

He said, "I guess I'll leave tomorrow."

I said, "I'd like to go with you."

He shook his head. "No, you don't need to go. I'll be back in a day or two."

I had to let that sink in. He didn't want me there. I was not going to be at the funeral services for my father-in-law. I didn't understand then and I don't understand now. I was in tears, so hurt I couldn't even ask why. I can only guess that Mick wanted to grieve alone. In his mind the funeral was only for his family, and that did not include me, not yet.

It did not occur to me to argue that I belonged there, that my place was with him. The decision was his and I accepted it. When he came back, the subject never came up.

Billy Martin and Mickey were roommates on the road, and when the team was at home we started spending most of our free time with Billy and his first wife, Lois. By August, Lois and I were both pregnant and the Yankees were on their way to an American League pennant and the World Series.

Suddenly, New York seemed an enchanting place. Mickey's leg had finally healed and Casey moved him into center field in late May. At the same time, Billy recovered from a cracked ankle and returned as the starter at second base, and the team took off.

Mickey batted .311 that season, with 23 home runs. I loved watching him play, and the Yankee fans were beginning to feel the same way. He had a grace, a presence about him that caught everyone's eye. When the Yankees needed something, a hit or a catch, I just knew that Mick would come through. And so many times, he did.

They met the Brooklyn Dodgers in the World Series, and Mick had a home run in the seventh and deciding game, off Joe Black, and he picked Jackie Robinson off second base. After the last game, Robinson came into the Yankee clubhouse and shook his hand. Mick was really impressed, and flattered.

They gave him a parade in Commerce when we got back, and the two of us sat in the back seat of an open convertible and waved to the crowds. Then they honored him at a banquet in the old Spartan Cafeteria, and Tom Greenwade, the scout who signed him, and Allie Reynolds, one of the Yankee pitching stars, were among the guests. Mick's mother, his brothers, and his sister were all in the crowd, beaming at him.

There are not many moments in your life when you are so happy you can cry. This was one of them. Mick was the center fielder on a world championship team. He had filled the spikes of Joe DiMaggio—leaving some room to grow.

Greenwade had discovered Mickey playing for a semipro team during his junior year in high school. He showed up the night of his graduation in the spring of 1949 to sign him to a minor league contract for the Yankees. When he offered him $400 a month, his father almost lost his temper. He told him Mickey could make that much in the mines and playing ball on weekends.

He was still a shortstop then, and Greenwade reflected on his weaknesses as a fielder. He said he was a little small—he hadn't filled out yet—and no one knew how he would hit when he went up against real pitchers. But he said he was willing to take a gamble. He sweetened the deal with a bonus of $1,100 and Mick signed.

Years later, someone asked Tom Greenwade about the night he discovered Mickey. He said, "I thought to myself, This is how Paul Krichell must have felt, the first time he saw Lou Gehrig."

The Yankees were now getting a pretty good return on their first investment.

That winter we built a new house across town from the one he had bought for his folks. Mick's World Series check came to $7,000, nearly as much as he made for the year. We put $16,000 in the house altogether, and my dad got us discount prices on all the lumber.

And Billy Martin called to tell us that Lois had given birth to a baby girl, and that she was filing for a divorce. I felt badly for them, but I have to admit that Billy's calls made me nervous. I liked him, but a lot less than Mickey did, and I had no plans to adopt him.

The second week in April 1953, our baby was born—a son. Mickey was in Brooklyn, where the Yankees were playing the Dodgers in an exhibition game. They announced it over the public address system:

"Now hitting, Number 7, Mickey Mantle . . . Mickey doesn't know it yet, but he just became the father of an eight-pound, twelve-ounce baby boy."

We named him Mickey Elvin, after his dad and grand-dad, and even though their middle names are different we stuck a junior on him. He was that freckle-faced, redhaired boy Mutt Mantle had wanted, but did not live to see.

I would never do that again, if I had it to do over. I think it must have been very hard growing up as Mickey Mantle Jr., but he handled it remarkably well.

One year, when he was about three, we were on a plane going to join his daddy in spring training. He was running up and down the aisle, the way little kids of that age love to do, arms and legs going in all directions. As he went by, a woman leaned out of her seat and asked, "What's your name, honey?"

He paused and said, "Mickey Mantle."

"Oh, isn't that cute?" sighed the woman. "He thinks he's Mickey Mantle, the baseball player."

It was a full month before the Yankees would let him get away so he could meet his first child. He adored Mickey Jr., and just marveled at the miracle of seeing his own face in miniature. I accepted the fact that he couldn't be with me for the birth of his son, but I hated that he had to return to New York after two days.

When you sign up to be a baseball wife, you forfeit your right to bitch about not having your husband at the hospital when you go into labor. That's part of the game—a phrase every baseball wife needs to keep handy.

Among the benefits of having a baby, one of the nicest for me was not having to return to the Concourse Plaza Hotel. Mickey rented a house for us in New Jersey, and we joined him in July. It was like starting all over again when I stepped off the plane with little Mickey in my arm, and felt his father embrace us both.

There was a whole new world out there, and everything came at you with the speed of a high, inside fastball. Mickey still wanted to be free to run and play, and I wanted to run with him. For the first six years, my parents helped raise Mickey Jr. I'll always be grateful for that.

The fans were starting to gasp at the distances of Mick's home runs. Early that season, he hit the home run at Griffith Park in Washington that left the field at the 391-foot mark, struck a beer sign on the football scoreboard, landed in the parking lot, and bounced into someone's back yard. Red Patterson, then the Yankee publicity man, walked it off and announced that the ball traveled 565 feet.

That was the birth of the so-called "tape-measure" home run, which became Mickey's trademark.

That fall they beat the Dodgers again in the World Series, this time in six games. To celebrate, Mick and I flew with Harold Youngman and his wife, Stella, to Havana, Cuba, as their guests.

We were on a new track and a faster one. In New York, all those bright lights beckoned to us. The plush night spots, like the Copacabana and the Latin Quarter, always had the red carpet out for the Yankee players. Some nights the wives were invited, some nights they were not. Mick was finding his way around New York. I had my hands full finding Mick.

One of my worst fears was realized that winter when Billy Martin drove all the way from Berkeley, California, to be our houseguest. Billy arrived in a new Cadillac he had been given as the star of the World Series.

Mick sensed that as much as he enjoyed Billy's company, this was not going to be a positive experience. One day, he admitted to me, "You know, if my dad were alive, he would take one look at Billy and tell him to get back in his frigging car and go back to California." Mutt would have known from looking at him that Billy Martin was not good for Mick.

All I saw of the two of them that winter was their backs going out the door. If they did all the hunting and fishing they claimed they were doing, the fish and quail population of Oklahoma and Missouri took a fearful beating.

At times, they were capable of being such juveniles, lovable, but childish. When their wives went on the road with them, Billy and Mickey would sometimes each sneak out to the window ledge and crawl around, peek into the other's room, and see what the other one was doing. One night they actually bumped heads.

But I have to make a confession. For a lot of years, I blamed Billy Martin as Mickey's drinking kept increasing, and his eye wandered, and he became so fidgety about staying home. Eventually, it dawned on me that Mickey made those choices. It wasn't Billy Martin's fault or Whitey Ford's fault or anyone else's.

It may have been a hard winter for Billy. His wife had left him and taken their little girl with her. Mickey helped him through a bad time, and I won't second-guess myself

A HERO ALL HIS LIFE

for letting Billy move in with us. Anyway, he wrecked his Cadillac, totaled it, trying to outrace Mickey to the bottom of a hill.

The Yankees missed the World Series in 1954, the year the Cleveland Indians won 111 games. It was a shock to me to learn that the World Series check wasn't automatic, that it wasn't part of our annual pay.

They were back the next year, lost to the Dodgers, and then arranged for the team to make a postseason tour of Japan, with a stop in Hawaii. My timing was terrible. I was pregnant again. Harold Youngman got to go with Mick in my place.

Whatever spending money the Yankees had advanced the players, Mick blew his in a poker game. The parties must have been a very high octane, because after a week in Japan he was ready to come home. He had Harold's secretary send a fake telegram to the front office, saying that I was about to give birth and Mickey was needed at home.

Two months later, I was still waiting to give birth. On Christmas Eve, one of our houseguests—we had them every winter now—left and walked off with Mick's house keys. I had taken Mickey Jr. and gone to my mother's to open some gifts. We stayed late and I let little Mickey spend the night there.

When I came home there was a drunken entourage standing around in the front yard. They couldn't get in the house and Mick was furious. He blamed me for locking him out and taking his key. I told him, "I don't know where your keys are." At that point, he grabbed me by the arm and pushed me aside. If I had fallen, I probably would have had the baby then and there.

The twins, Ray and Roy, were in the group, and they were visibly upset by what they saw. They went home and told his mom and the next day she climbed all over him. That was the first time he had embarrassed me in front of other people.

Our second son, David, arrived two days later, on December 26, 1955. The Yankees knew then that Mick had pulled a cute one. They deducted what he would have been paid if he had stayed on the trip. I guess we could have claimed I was in labor for eight weeks, but we had made up and were too happy to argue—with the Yankees or with each other.

We were coming into what I thought then were the magical years. Mick won his Triple Crown in 1956, was the league's Most Valuable Player that year and the next, and saw his salary jump to $65,000. He was the toast of New York, and I don't mean to be trite. There is nothing quite like it, the status, the attention, the power of being a New York icon. It really is true: If you can make it there, you can make it anywhere.

New York was still a three-team town (and with a dozen newspapers.) There was the personal rivalry the fans and the press whipped up between the center fielders, Willie Mays and Duke Snider and Mick. It was a fantasy time. We were having our babies, going to some really neat places, and, in my imagination, having breakfast at Tiffany's. I thought I had the perfect marriage. *Look at me,* I thought. *I'm married to Mickey Mantle.* Who wouldn't want to be married to Mickey Mantle? I know I did. I loved being Mrs. Mickey Mantle.

They knew him on Park Avenue and Madison Avenue,

and they were singing his name on Broadway. Everywhere we went, his admirers sent over bottles of champagne or whatever he was drinking. That covered a wide range. And I was trying my best to keep up.

I'm still not quite sure how Mickey Charles Mantle, out of Spavinaw and Commerce, Oklahoma, became a New York guy, but he did. And it scared the wits out of me. He was one of a fairly small group of people who, at what they did, were symbols of making it big in New York. Babe Ruth. Jack Dempsey. Frank Sinatra. Mayor Jimmy Walker. Joe DiMaggio. And the Mick. They were huge in New York, which is the place where being huge really counted.

I don't know if that New York still exists. The city can still manufacture heroes, but it no longer turns out the kind of idols people let into their hearts, and never let them out.

When we were there in the fifties, you still found a lot of Damon Runyon and Walter Winchell in New York. Mick came along when the fans still wanted to believe in heroes, heroes who had big talents and big appetites and big flaws. But, in the end, the hero had to come through. Mickey could do that.

He led the league in homers in 1958 and the Yankees beat the Milwaukee Braves in the World Series. And our third son, Billy Giles Mantle, was born the week of Thanksgiving. His father was in Kerrville, Texas, hunting deer with Billy Martin—Mick named his new son after him. The middle name was my dad's.

The baby was born in Joplin, and my parents were there for me one more time. Billy would grow up to be the smallest of the boys, and that was unfortunate, because he had his godfather's temper. He was always testing, always needing to prove something. He favored my side of the family, which was a bit unfair, since the others all so strongly resembled their dad. He had that interesting combination of a quick temper, a reckless disregard for his own safety, and a gentle and generous heart. But we can only wonder what the mix would have been if Billy had not developed Hodgkin's at nineteen.

We had begun to notice a sad pattern by now. Our fourth son, Danny, was born in March 1960 at Baylor University Hospital in Dallas. Mick would spend his final days there. But he was in spring training in Fort Lauderdale when Danny came into the world.

I wasn't angry with him, at least, not unreasonably so. I knew that you don't change the rules in the middle of the game, and our rule was that baseball always came first. It always had. And one way or another, it always would.

I couldn't claim that I was lonely anymore. I had our boys, and they were adorable, they were fun, and they were proud of the daddy they caught glimpses of four months out of the year.

Chapter 3

Pride of the Yankees

W HEN I THINK ABOUT THE FIFTIES, I REMEMBER seeing the newsreels before the feature at the movies. A deep, doomsday voice would remind us that "Time marches on!" It surely did.

Billy Martin had been traded to Kansas City in the middle of the 1957 season, at least partly because George Weiss, the team's cranky general manager, did not like the influence he had on Mickey.

The Yankees also had a good young prospect to replace him at second base in Bobby Richardson. It doesn't take long to learn that ball clubs will tolerate a player's mischief, his ego, his rebellion—if they don't have someone who can fill his spot.

Billy's departure hit Mickey hard. They had been roommates for nearly seven years on the road, and nearly as much in the off-season. A lot less was said about it, but the trade included Ralph Terry, another pal Mick would miss. Ralph was from the same part of Oklahoma we were. He was a few years younger, but had pitched against Commerce and Mick's cousin, Max Mantle, in the Lucky Seven High School Conference.

At one point, there was talk of an all-Mantle outfield, but sometimes fate gives you a life and sometimes a kick. The twins, Roy and Ray, were both fine athletes and signed with the Yankees. Both hit over .300 in Class D ball, but an injury ended Roy's career. Ray was drafted and spent two years in the army. When he came home from the army he no longer had the same desire for the game. I think the idea of playing without his twin had something to do with his loss of interest.

In return for Billy and Ralph, the Yankees got Harry Simpson and Ryne Duren. I never heard Mick say whether it was a good trade or a bad one, but the Yankees kept right on winning pennants.

Losing Billy Martin as a running mate, and gaining a family, did not make Mickey a more responsible person, but it slowed him down some. Each summer, I would pile the kids into the car and drive east—I was afraid of flying, a fear I have not completely overcome.

We always rented a house in New Jersey. Several of the players with families did the same. You had to go across the river to find a house you could afford. We didn't look for anything fancy. With four little boys, believe me, no one was going to let you rent their dream house.

The last house we rented in New Jersey was in Fort Lee, owned by a man who taught at a college in the New York area, and his wife. They owned cats, and I discovered kitty poop behind the curtains and under the furniture, left there for so long it was petrified. The boys developed boils, and I moved us into a motel while we aired the place out. I scrubbed that house for a solid month before I would let the kids eat in it.

There were no headboards on any of the beds, and on the wall in the master bedroom there was a large, round grease spot just above our heads. No detergent or chemical I could find was able to remove it. I came to look upon it as one would a freak of nature. Some of the players dropped by one night, and I invited them to view it.

Ralph Terry, who had rejoined the team in 1959, stood at the foot of the bed and was briefly lost in concentration. "Merlyn," he asked, "have you noticed the painting over the bed?"

At the same instant, Mick and I turned to look at the painting. Then we looked at each other and burst out laughing. The painting was of a couple making love. I had been too preoccupied with the grease spot to even notice.

Renting a home is no inconvenience for the players of today, with the megabucks most of them are paid. They simply buy a second house, or a third. With us, it was always an adventure.

The players had to be at the park three hours before the game. If they played at night, four or five players would get up a car pool and take the George Washington Bridge into New York. Mick would be back around midnight, unwind with a cold beer and go to bed.

Day games meant you had a chance to stay in town, take in a show, or meet friends for dinner. But if the team had just come off a road trip, I knew Mick would be tired of eating in restaurants and we'd usually have dinner at home.

Those few summers when the kids were little may have been as close to having a normal family life as we ever knew. I didn't mind missing a few parties. I felt guilty if I had to leave the boys with a babysitter. But I had slipped, unknowingly, into a trap. When we did go out, I would have at least two or three drinks before we left the house and a roadie to go—one for the car. By then I would feel smarter, surer, almost interesting.

I don't think I had a clue yet that we were, each in our own way, losing control. No one suggested then that Mick had a drinking problem. When he had too much he was a happy drunk, and that seemed to soften the consequences. There were episodes.

One night, we met Clete Boyer and his wife at a club in New York, then went on to dinner at a nice restaurant in New Jersey. Mick was feeling his oats, and he and Clete were quietly getting loaded. I had not been drinking that night. I base that on the fact that my memory of the evening is still so sharp. I went to the powder room. When I came back he pulled my chair out from under me and I fell hard to the floor. This was his idea of a prank. Even though I understood this, I was never able to get through to him: there was something sadistic about that kind of physical humor. If nothing else, my pride was hurt.

I started to cry, announced I was going home, and got into the car.

Clete jumped in the front seat, trying to calm me down. I was pulling out of the parking lot when Mick stepped outside. I floorboarded it—Clete's jaw dropped—and missed Mick by a hair. I had *tried* to hit him. He stumbled out of the way at the last second.

Then I did take a deep breath, and everyone got into the car. When we reached our house, I went inside and Mick passed out on the lawn. I left him there. Sometime during the night, he came to bed.

That incident frightened us both, and Mickey stopped drinking for a week, maybe even two. We went to dinner with the Berras, and we always found it easy to relax around Carmen and Yogi. She was a beauty, and still is, and was the first of the wives to help me acquire a sense of style. We loved them both, dearly.

Mick was drinking straight vodka on the rocks. As we got into our car, Yogi called out, "Merlyn, I wouldn't let him drive, if I was you." I begged Mick for the keys and he just laughed.

We had a new Oldsmobile and he was doing seventy. When he wouldn't slow down, I whacked the side of his head with my purse. He reached over to try to take the purse away from me and the next thing I knew we were halfway up a telephone pole. My head cracked the windshield and the rearview mirror just creased my scalp. At the hospital they treated me for a concussion, and it took several stitches to close the wound in my head. But I didn't pass out and I knew I wasn't seriously hurt. As self-suffering as this may sound, my only worry was that the story would get in the papers and Mick would be in trouble.

As luck would have it, the officer who investigated the accident was our next-door neighbor. There were no charges filed and not a word appeared in the press. Mick had to pay $400 for the damages to the telephone pole, and the next day he played in both games of a double-header.

Twenty years later, he still referred to his drinking as if it were one long fraternity romp. In his autobiography, he mentioned Ryne Duren's disclosure that he was an alcoholic. Duren went through treatment and eventually become a counselor on substance abuse.

"I used to run around with Ryne a lot," said Mick. "But, thank God, I was lucky enough to have had a greater tolerance . . ."

The bigger he became as a star, the less secure Mickey felt as a person. His mood swings were wild. He could be laughing and having fun one minute, snarling and swearing the next.

A few of the players were invited to Las Vegas after one World Series, and there was a dinner that included Mrs. Del Webb, whose late husband had owned the Yankees with Bob Topping. It was Del Webb who stepped in and gave Mick a raise to $65,000 after George Weiss threatened to trade him to Cleveland. I was glad we had a chance to tell Mrs. Webb how much we appreciated the kindness of her husband. I was glad right up to the moment Mick, who was snockered, soaked his napkin in a water glass, then threw it in my face.

The other guests pretended nothing had happened. A wife with a suspicious mind might have thought her husband was trying to drive her in tears to their room so he could go off and play. I can't explain it. I don't think he could, either.

That was how we rode out the rough seas of our marriage. Off and on, I would block them out because I wanted people to like him. I wanted them to see him as modest and gallant, the lovable Mickey Mantle. He was all of that.

During his playing days, he traveled in the winter because we needed the money. It wasn't only the money. He felt obligated to go to banquets, to meet the fans who didn't get to see big league teams up close. One year he went to Alaska with Bob Hope to entertain the troops, and got home just before Christmas. Those were neat trips. The kids and I still have the snowshoes he brought back from Alaska.

He was thoughtful and even extravagant about gifts. But Christmas was a complicated time for him. As a child, there were years when the Mantles didn't have much, if anything, to put under their tree.

One year, Harold Youngman told Mick that I needed a mink stole. Our anniversary was coming up, just two days before Christmas. "The hell she does," he said. "I can't afford it." But he thought about it, and when I opened my present it was a mink stole that cost $2,500. This was when I was about to give birth to David, the Christmas we had our confrontation on the lawn. I have to give him credit, he knew how to kiss and make up. A mink stole was one of the things every woman dreamed about in the fifties.

Our first Christmas in Dallas, in 1957, he went to Neiman-Marcus and bought me a diamond and sapphire charm. The engraving on the charm said, "I Love You More Today, But Less than Tomorrow."

He was the sole owner of a new bowling alley in Dallas, and he liked the idea of living in a city with excellent air service and within driving distance of Joplin and Commerce.

(We had no way of knowing that the bowling boom was about to end. That investment was a disaster.)

The most confidence he ever showed in me was when he let me go to Dallas and pick out a new house. I fell in love with one in the new Preston Hollow section of Dallas—four bedrooms, three and a half baths on an acre of land for $59,500. It was the first house I looked at, and it was *my* home for thirty-six years. We added a pool and a cabana, and I turned the garage into a trophy room, but over the years it needed little in the way of updating. We could travel, be in Florida for spring training or gone all summer, and the minute I walked in the front door it was like, Ahhhh, this is mine. The dirt here is my dirt. I'm safe now.

The boys have their own vague memories of those years. But I remember them as four chubby little boys with crew cuts and short pants, running wild through the stands at Yankee Stadium, playing with the sons of Yogi and Billy and Roger Maris. Sometimes, loaded down with pop and hot dogs and Cracker Jack, worn out from a half-day of chasing each other, they would fall asleep in the locker room while the game was going on. Mick would sneak back there between innings just to look at them, close together, heads or shoulders touching, curled up like kittens in a basket.

Only Mickey Jr. was old enough to sense what was happening in the stadium when Mick did something great. But they liked it when the crowd cheered, and roared in that special way. They didn't like it when the crowd booed, although they were not sure what the booing meant.

What I did impress upon them was the importance of

leaving Daddy alone when he came home if the Yankees had lost or he had struck out four times or some equally unforgivable act. I was never able to look at Mick on the field with a critical eye. I wouldn't have known how. But I knew how much he wanted to be the best, and how hard he tried, and how he tied himself in knots if things were not going well.

All during his career, the Yankees pressed him to do two things: play to the crowd a little more, and cut down on his strikeouts.

He resisted the first and was just incapable of the second. He raced around the bases with his head down when he hit a homer, so he wouldn't embarrass the pitcher. It was hard for him to tip his hat when they cheered, a small gesture, but one that struck him as a kind of pandering.

In the spring of his second or third year, Ty Cobb, the player most regarded as the greatest of all time, came to see him. I don't know if the Yankees suggested this, or if Cobb was simply impressed with his potential. He told Mickey he liked the fact that he didn't hesitate to drag a bunt for a base hit. He encouraged him to do more of it. He thought this was a way to reduce his strikeouts. (A movie about Cobb was released in 1995, and it showed him to be a real hellraiser. He could have given Mick some lessons off the field, too.)

His advice was fine and well taken, but the Yankees didn't want Mick hitting singles. And all too soon, the injuries to his legs had cost him a step and made it difficult for him to make a sharp cut.

Then Mick, on his own, sought out the great Ted Williams for advice. Williams, who regarded hitting as an art and a science, talked to him about how he used his hips, and keeping his elbows in, and a few other pointers. When Mick came home with more than two things to think about, it gave him a migraine. So he forgot Cobb and he forgot Williams. He swung at every pitch like it was the last one he might ever see, as he always had.

In eight seasons he struck out more than one hundred times, and in four others he was in the nineties.

I don't have a press credential, so I probably shouldn't be getting into what some might call inside baseball. But the above references were meant to show that Mick wanted to improve, and he wanted to be popular. But he had to be what he was. Most of the time, that was more than enough—for his teammates and for the fans who really loved him. It wasn't always enough for Mick.

If people ask me about his records, I have to look it up (or ask the boys). I know Mick led the league in home runs in 1958 and 1960. But in the year of his greatest output he came in second. In 1961, he hit fifty-four homers and had a historic, season-long rivalry with Roger Maris to break Babe Ruth's record.

Roger won. He hit his sixty-first homer on the last day of the season against the Red Sox. An infected hip side-lined Mick for nearly two weeks in late September, and it became a one-man race. Mick rooted for Roger and was truly thrilled for him.

They had gone back and forth during the first three quarters of the season, and it was clear that Mickey was the people's choice. In a way it was weird. They sometimes booed Maris for hitting a home run. But if anyone was going to break Ruth's record, the fans had decided it should be Mickey Mantle. He was part of the Yankee tradition, the successor to DiMaggio.

Maris had already played for two other teams before he joined the Yankees. It was hard to believe, but he was even more shy than Mick. He didn't smile much. He was quiet and reserved, and the fans saw him as cold and indifferent.

Mick actually tried to help him with the press and with the public. Boy, talk about a role reversal. It took his duel with Maris to get the fans to appreciate what he had done, and their ovations seemed to say, "We should have told you sooner, but it's not too late. We love you, Mick."

His drinking wasn't an issue when he was having his big seasons. But changes were taking place all around him. The Yankees fired Casey Stengel after they lost the 1960 World Series to the Pirates. Ralph Houk was moved into the manager's job.

Casey wasn't fired because they lost the Series but because of his age, and he didn't leave gladly. "I will never make the mistake of being seventy again," he said.

Stengel had been a father figure to Mick for most of their time together, but Houk's approach was actually better for him. He didn't treat Mick as a son, but as a man. He named him the team captain and asked him to take an active role as the leader of the team. He made it clear that the other players looked up to him and would listen if he offered any help, or criticism.

If he was using psychology, it was done in a nice, subtle way. Mickey had been an example to his teammates, and that was not always a good thing. They saw him playing hurt, fine. They saw him drink till he dropped, not so fine. So Ralph was wise not to ask him to lead by example.

But nearly all of the players he had broken in with were gone, and now so was Casey. Mick turned thirty in 1961, and after ten years in the league he should have been coming into his prime. But he worried about what toll the injuries had taken, and how long he could continue to play at a level that would satisfy his own enormous pride.

He needed baseball for a lot of reasons. In one odd respect, it interrupted his drinking. Like many players, Mick would quit drinking a few days before spring training opened. I always thought this went back to their days as high school jocks. But something inside them said it was time to get into shape. Some guys would quit smoking. This was like a superstition—you don't break training.

So Mick stopped drinking. Whatever the logic, staying sober for even a few weeks certainly gave his system a rest and helped him last as long as he did. Of course, when he decided he was in shape or the season opened, whichever came first, he started drinking again.

His will was strong enough, then, not to drink when he thought it might interfere with his performance. But he wasn't an impartial judge of when that was. There was no doubt now that he was famous, and for the rest of his days he would feel confusion about how to handle it.

In 1962, he made a cameo appearance in a movie called *That Touch of Mink,* starring Doris Day and Cary Grant. The same year, Roger Maris and Mick were paid $25,000 apiece for three days' work in a silly baseball film called *Safe at Home.* The whole family flew to Fort Lauderdale for the shooting, and Mickey Jr. and David were given bit parts.

The movie was about a boy, a fan of Mickey Mantle,

who made promises to his Little League team he couldn't keep, so he ran away from home. After the boys had finished their parts, the director said he thought David might have some acting talent, and he offered to give us the name of an agent.

Mick said, "No, thanks. One star in the family is enough." I can't be sure that he thought the man was serious. Or, if he did, he didn't want to risk having the boys exposed to the kind of pressures he himself was still struggling to tame.

But I thought there was a shadow on little David's face, just a hint of disappointment.

By 1963, I decided to stop hauling the boys halfway across the country each summer. In the first place, they didn't want to go. Junior was ten, David was seven, Billy was five, and Danny, three. I made up my mind the previous summer, when we rented a home next door to a family that had a swimming pool One day, I looked out the kitchen window and noticed all four of the boys, in their bathing trunks, hanging over the fence, watching the other kids in the neighborhood swim. You could hear the laughter and splashing coming from the other yard.

I asked through the window why they weren't in the pool. One of them said, "They told us we couldn't come in." I don't know why the boys were snubbed, but it hurt them, and me, very much. If we were home in Dallas, they could have been swimming in their own back yard.

The other factor was the tension the season placed on them. They had to walk on eggshells if Mick struck out a couple of times. A bad day at the plate equaled a bad night at the plate. We would eat dinner in something close to silence. And when you're five years old, or three, this is defying nature.

When Mick came off a long road trip, we all went on a kind of special alert. It was like the return of the king. I spent hours preparing dinner. The house had to be immaculate. The boys were scrubbed and combed. We even washed the dog.

This display wasn't hard to explain. I was looking for solid rock on which our marriage could stand. I just wanted to please him. I loved him. I adored him. I've been told that he was my addiction.

So I started looking forward to the day he no longer played baseball. Mick did not. He lived in dread of that time.

The worst point in his career was the spring of 1968. I don't think I ever saw him with nerves so raw, so glum, so edgy. He was sleeping poorly. He wasn't drinking more, but he was eating less.

Yogi Berra had come and gone as manager, after the Yankees won the pennant but lost the World Series in 1964 to the Cardinals. Johnny Keane, the manager of the team that beat them, took over and lasted less than two years.

Ralph Houk was back, and he had asked Mick to play first base, hoping it would be easier on his wobbly knees. He was worried sick that he couldn't do it, that he would embarrass himself. During this time he was moody and very quiet, but after a few games he did well. Everything looked brighter, except that he couldn't turn back the clock.

In February, he talked about retiring. The cartilage was

completely gone in his right knee, just bone on bone. When you asked him how bad the pain was, he would say, "Not bad. It's like a toothache."

Then one day he drove past a high school baseball diamond, and stopped his car and watched the kids play for a few minutes. Then this great desire swept over him and he made up his mind to go to Florida. Just like that.

He was really hard to live with that winter until he went to camp, played in a few games, and convinced himself he could do it. I'm sure I only had half an idea of what he was going through. He was thirty-six—he would turn thirty-seven in October—and the Yankees were a bad ball club.

Every time he came to bat now, the Yankee fans practically gave a standing ovation. It wasn't all that different in parks where the fans had hated the Yankees. But the cheers and the applause sounded off-key to him. "It's all sentiment," he said. "I'm not sure I like that. They sure as hell aren't cheering me for my batting average."

It wasn't a good season, not the way he wanted to say good-bye. As it turned out, they still needed him in the outfield and he played only thirteen games at first base. His batting average dropped to an all-time low of .237.

To make matters worse, he finished with a career average of .298. Mick always thought of himself as a .300 hitter. That was a real disappointment to him.

He hit his last home run on September 20, 1968, off Jim Lonborg of the Red Sox, the 536th of his career. When he came home that fall he told me he was through, but the Yankees still sent him a contract for the 1969 season, at a salary of $100,000. He let it sit around unsigned, and I wasn't sure what he would end up doing. Neither was he.

The Yankees told him they still needed him. The league needed him. There was an expansion team in Seattle and they wanted Mickey Mantle coming to town with the Yankees.

He felt he owed it to everybody, including himself, to see if he could go one more year with dignity. He went to Florida a few days early to work out, and see if his legs would hold up. He confirmed what he already knew. He couldn't run anymore.

At the press conference the next day, he said it simply, with no candy coating: "I can't hit when I need to. I can't steal a base when I want to. I can't get from first to third when I have to. It was time to quit trying."

Students of grammar would probably have pointed out that he shouldn't have ended those sentences with all those prepositions. But he wasn't ending a sentence, he was ending a way of life.

In June 1969, the Yankees retired his number at a ceremony in Yankee Stadium. All of us were there, on the field, and it was a scene that tugged at your heart. Mickey had complained all night about not knowing what he would say. He accepted a plaque from Joe DiMaggio, and when he stepped to the microphone he thanked the right people and said the right thing. He even managed to add a footnote to the most dramatic moment in all of the Yankees' tradition.

He said, "When Lou Gehrig made his farewell speech, I never understood how a man could say it was the happiest day of his life, when he knew he was dying. Now I understand."

Back in Dallas, we had started on what we thought

would be a new life, or at least a new chapter. In some ways, it hadn't changed at all.

Mick was trying to help get the new restaurant business, Mickey Mantle's Country Cookin', off and running. He was a partner in a men's clothing line, out of Knoxville, Tennessee.

But he was still on the road most of the time. The boys and I were not seeing much more of him than we had when he played ball. His drinking had taken a leap, and I was finding it harder to accept his excuses when he came home after three or four days on the road, and his shirts reeked of perfume and had lipstick on the collar.

The thing is, I wanted to believe him and I usually just dropped the subject. I tried to separate whatever happened out of town, what I didn't know or hear about, from the life we had as a family. Mick was one of those men who wanted to be married, but only part-time.

We were doing all right financially, but that didn't keep us from feeling that we were just one wrong move from being broke. We hadn't put any money away, and none of his new deals came with a guarantee.

The funny thing is, we felt a certain security with the Yankees because he had been paid $100,000 in each of his last seven seasons, and most of the time we could count on a World Series check as an annual bonus. Yet Mick and his teammates were always on a year-to-year contract, and they had to prove themselves again every season.

For myself, I was thrilled to have him out of baseball, and kept thinking we would have more time with him when some of the ventures panned out. Mick made a very fortunate move when he hired a young attorney, Roy True, to review his business dealings. More than that, Roy became a kind of guardian angel for all of us.

The boys were growing up, and I believe Mick really wanted to find time for them. But if one of them was playing baseball or football, he couldn't sit in the stands and watch them. People would just form a line, or surround him, to get autographs. He didn't know what they were doing in school, and seldom asked. They came to him for money, which he gave freely, but not advice. He told them to get haircuts.

When Mick retired, a big chunk of his self-esteem went out the window. I question whether he ever had much to begin with. People may find it amazing that I could say such a thing; here is someone who was celebrated, who was a hero to a generation of baseball fans, and who rubbed elbows with the rich and famous. But Mick was hiding behind alcohol. When he stopped hitting home runs, the only time he had any self-esteem was after a drink or two.

I tried to get him to talk about what he missed, what he needed, what he wanted from his family. I thought it was so revealing when he told *Sports Illustrated* in 1994, "I'd never thought about anything serious in my life for a continuous period of days and weeks until I checked into the Betty Ford Center . . ."

Deep down, Mick was scared half to death of people. I could see that in him because I was, too. You think, If I'm friendly and outgoing they might find out what I am really about. So you try to keep it inside and give them only what you want them to have and no more. That's what Mick did.

Both of us were in total denial about what was happening to all of us. As they grew into their teens, the boys were floundering. They were bored with school. They were reckless in cars, starting to drink, getting into dope. When I tried to tell Mick, he was shocked that they would mess with dope. It was something he could not see himself doing.

He argued with them. They argued right back. The boys thought smoking a joint or snorting cocaine was no worse than getting high on booze. And Mick would reply, "Yeah, but it's against the law." They said, "Yeah, but at one time so was booze." Around and around they went, until Mick would get bored with the argument and walk away.

We got through those years mainly by ignoring our problems, and when they couldn't be ignored we would call Roy True.

Mick was consistent about making it home for holidays and our anniversary. He always sent me pink roses. For our nineteenth wedding anniversary, he bought me a diamond and sapphire bracelet. On the card that came with it, he had written, "I hope the next nineteen years are as happy as the first nineteen."

We only missed it by two. We lived together for more than thirty-six years.

Chapter 4

Keeping Up with Mick

I LOVED MICKEY MANTLE SO MUCH THAT I WANTED TO crawl inside him and live underneath his skin. I wanted to control everything he did.

It took me too long to understand that this was more love than Mick wanted or could accept. It was a sick kind of love. I was suffocating him.

So we rocked along for quite a few years, with me hoping things would get better and Mick unable to admit that anything was wrong. The truth is, I didn't know that I was part of the problem. If there was any unpleasantness, I drank. But I didn't consider myself addicted.

The main result of my drinking was to get into arguments with Mick. I knew that my drinking was having an effect on what was happening in our lives.

I don't know if Mick was alarmed by the way his drinking escalated. It was after I was in recovery that I could see it myself. I watched him go from three-day benders to week-long benders and, at the last, every day. But at intervals he made an effort to control it by using his own sports psychology. He would declare what he called a "time-out," and go on the wagon for two or three months. He would play golf at Preston Trails, come home, have dinner, watch TV, and fall asleep on the sofa. During the time-outs we had some semblance of a normal life.

When he was drinking, I would sit up many a night staring out the window, waiting for him to come home, scared stiff that he had been in a wreck and killed someone, or himself. The relief I felt when he walked in the door was overwhelming, followed seconds later by a desire to strangle him. An anger was building in me that I could not relate to the person I was. Thoughts of violence are not unique. You hear the same story from just about anyone who has experienced alcoholism.

A point begs to be made here: No matter how much he drank, Mick never slapped or hit or tried to hurt me. As close as he came was the time he grabbed my arm and swung me around, when I was nine months pregnant with David. His temper was of the barking, not the biting, kind.

I could push the bad times aside because it is very easy to get caught up in the American way of fame. I was bored, and when I did get to be a part of it, I enjoyed the lifestyle.

So often I didn't know whether to laugh or cry. Once, when David was seven years old, Mick came home drunk and was bouncing into the walls.

David watched him with big eyes, then looked at me and said, "I'm going to write a story about him someday."

Mick was a true alcoholic. He never seemed to have a

hangover. I can remember only one time when he stayed home because he was hung over so badly. He was lying on the sofa in the den, when the piano tuner showed up. We liked this little man, who had a slight Hungarian accent, and we always let him tune our piano. No one ever played it, but we kept it wonderfully tuned. That day, he was happily carrying out his work and you kept hearing the same sound: "plink . . . plink . . . plink." Finally, there was a cry from the couch: "Merlyn, I'll pay that guy any amount of money he wants, but get him out of here." So I paid him and he left.

The way I looked at it, I was raising five boys, including Mick, all during the seventies, until one by one they began to go out on their own—including Mick. But no matter how turbulent our relations were at a given time, we were a clannish family. We usually went out to dinner together when Mick was in town, and we always had a family Christmas.

I would spend all day cooking and he would make the eggnog. I'm not sure what he put in it, vodka, bourbon, rum, anything in the bar. Honestly, it was so strong that no one could drink it except him. The guests did sample it, however, and before I could get the turkey on the table everyone would be drunk. I finally put a stop to it. I said, "There is no more eggnog in this house on Christmas. If there is, I'm not cooking." I gave them other Yuletide options, vodka and cranberry juice, or wine. No eggnog.

Mickey was sober the day his playfulness nearly resulted in a lethal accident. We were unpacking the car after a trip, and he took his handgun out of the glove compartment. He always kept a gun in the car, in case of a robbery. Mick and the boys enjoyed hunting, and our homes at times resembled an armory.

In one of his kidding-around moods, he pointed the gun at me. I said, "Mick, don't do that. Don't ever do that."

He said, "Why? It's not loaded." To prove it, he held the gun straight up and pulled the trigger. And the gun went off. The blood drained from his face. He said, "My God, nobody would ever have believed that it was an accident, would they?"

I said, "Of course not. Not if you shoot someone at point-blank range. Now will you put it away?"

He quickly did. He spent a good part of the day reflecting on how close he came to facing a grand jury, or worse. I don't know why I was unshaken by it. I guess it goes back to the old saying, God looks after fools and drunks.

You can't wallow in regrets, but I wish I could have found the honesty or the will to seek help in the late seventies. I believe so much heartache might have been averted, and our family's renewal might have started earlier.

Mick and I were in total denial about what was happening to us and our sons. I really had no idea what I needed, or where to find it. The good times, partying, getting drunk, having guests pass out in our home, counting the holes burned in the carpet or the sofa the next day, this is the way we lived.

Three events, in a span of eight years, made it all but impossible to maintain the illusion of order in the Mantle family. In 1977, Billy was diagnosed with Hodgkin's disease, and thus began a battle that consumed him and, at times, each of us for the next seventeen years. Billy would have caught the eye of any mother or father. We saw the wholesome boy turn into the troubled young adult. We lived with his anxieties and saw him waste away.

Weakened by the cancer, hooked on the drugs that eased his pain, weakened by alcohol and the hardships he drifted into, Billy's heart gave out at thirty-six. I felt like my heart was broken, and I had so much guilt because I might have done so much more. But I know in my heart that I did the best I could.

That shock was impossible to separate from the next event, which took place in 1982. I discovered the first in what I learned was a string of Mick's affairs. In 1985, I had a mild stroke, stress related.

I'm not sure I can be totally honest about all that happened during these years and the ones that immediately followed. I tell myself that this is when my drinking got out of hand, but those were days when I easily fooled myself. Friends who had been in a twelve-step program listened to my complaints, and looked into my eyes and asked, "Merlyn, are you sure you're not an alcoholic?"

Who? Me? The question didn't offend me. The support I needed was to help me help my family. They were the ones with the problem. Now Mick had brought his problem home, where I could no longer ignore it.

I don't feel any purpose is served by getting into the gritty details. In 1982, the woman was from Dallas and some of my friends had seen them together. Mick had given her a job as his "secretary," and she traveled with him to card shows and to Atlantic City, where he had been hired as a sports host for the Claridge Hotel. He took the job because we needed the extra money for Billy's medical bills.

This was one of the conflicts in Mick. The caring father in him would surface, even as the considerate husband wandered.

It was in Atlantic City that I met her. At first I didn't think anything of it. I was told she worked for the Claridge. Many of the hotels had offices and secretaries in Dallas, so that didn't strike me as unusual. What did strike me as unusual was when I realized we had a suite, with two bedrooms and a parlor, and she was in the other bedroom.

Then she started to show up uninvited to parties at our home, and she seemed to have Mick's car more than he did. When she showed up at one of our parties, Mick said she only wanted to know if she could borrow *my* car. I found out later that she was putting pressure on him to leave me, and threatened to tell me of the affair if she didn't get her way.

Mickey no longer was bothering to conceal his romances. I was getting my nose rubbed in it. My anger was becoming uncontrollable. I was spending weeks at a time with Billy in Houston, where he was undergoing chemo treatment for his cancer.

As we drank our way through the eighties, Mick ended that affair and moved on to the next one. He met her at the Claridge as well. He repeated the story proudly. She was with one of the hotel's high rollers, who had played golf with Mick in the afternoon. That night he was at a table where the dice were hot, and she was bored and ready for dinner.

He called Mick over and asked if he would do him a favor. "I don't want to leave the table," he said. "Would you take her to dinner for me and entertain her?" That may have been the last the high roller ever saw of her.

I knew none of this at the time. The two affairs over-lapped by a few months. One or two of the boys usually traveled with him, too, so that put them squarely in the middle. They were old enough to drink with him now, and they considered it their duty to protect him at home. When I found out, they said they hated lying to me. But they jus-tified it by thinking they were shielding me from being hurt.

I had gone to Nashville with Mick for a charity golf tournament. That night, Mick went out before the awards banquet and didn't come back until six o'clock the next morning. I found out a few days later that he had spent the night with the wife of a well-known country singer.

This was in addition to the affairs he was having, the one in Dallas and the woman who replaced her. We were going on to Joplin for a family Christmas in 1985. It was also our anniversary, a time made even more strange and melancholy because a week earlier he had attended the funeral of Roger Maris, who had died of cancer. He was feeling sad and remorseful. At our home in Joplin, we got into a fight. It started over the one-night stand in Nashville, and moved on to the woman in Dallas. When I had gotten up enough steam, I threw a wine bottle at his head.

"Dammit, Merlyn," he said, "there's already somebody else and you're still fighting with me about the last one." He got into his car and left and no one saw or heard from him for several days, until we were all back in Dallas.

I decided, if he needed someone who parked her butt on a barstool and drank with him all night, I could be that person. I started to travel with him more, but I knew I couldn't be a guard dog the rest of my life.

Something had to give, and it turned out to be me. I suffered a mild stroke. My blood pressure was astronomical. They kept me in the hospital for three or four days, put me through a series of tests, and found that an artery in the back of my neck was blocked. The doctor put me on medication for my blood pressure, and blood thinners for the artery. The stroke was mild enough to serve as an early warning. It enabled me to postpone for a decade a heart problem that would result in my surgery in 1993.

Mick was on a book tour, promoting his autobiography, and he was wonderful. He canceled the next few stops and flew right home. He was there for me, trying to make up for what had happened outside our marriage.

Once I was out of the hospital, I made one of the worst mistakes of my life. I couldn't forgive him. This was where my illness came in. If I had been getting help for myself, I might have been able to forgive him and things might have turned out differently.

I argued with him constantly. The arguing turned into fights. And I probably drove him away. I wasn't mentally ready yet for any kind of recovery. If I had been, I would have handled everything differently. You don't try to change the other person. Now I know. I didn't then.

He left home and came back twice. He was gone three months and one night he called me, crying, wanting to come back home. I never questioned him, didn't ask why. I welcomed him back with open arms. I even went to his apartment to pick him up. He was sitting on the curb waiting for me. He stayed six weeks, and during that time Billy went into treatment for substance abuse in Arizona at The Meadows. I went to Arizona for family week. There were meetings the entire week. I heard things like, "The family becomes as sick as the alcoholic." It went right over my head. Two months later, I was in recovery. Our reconciliation was short-lived. I knew it wasn't going to work.

We were together at his fantasy camp in Florida, Mickey Mantle's Week of Dreams, in between his leaving home and coming back. While we were having dinner one night, he asked one of the waitresses for her phone number. Later, she called me aside and told me about it.

That started one of the longest, loudest fights we ever had. We went back to our room and the first thing I did was take off the pretty dress I was wearing and put on a sweatsuit. I was getting freed up to fight. The next thing I did was pick up a bar stool and throw it at him. He ducked, and it hit a glass-topped coffee table. The glass didn't break, but Mick hardly noticed. He just sort of fell backward and was sprawled there, drunk, on the bed.

I was furious. I jumped on the bed and straddled him. I started slapping his face, from one side to the next, like a windshield wiper. All the boys were in the room and they were unsure how to go about pulling me off him.

When he covered up his face, I balled up my fist and punched him around the head. "Ow, ow," he kept whining. "Hey, Merlyn, that hurts."

There is no way to excuse my behavior that night. My anger had simply erupted. I was screaming and yelling. The boys were running around in circles, trying to figure out how to stop me without having to physically restrain me.

Finally, the people in the next room called the police. I don't blame them a bit. The officers were quite nice. They separated us and made me go to a room by myself. I took Billy's room, and he moved in with one of his brothers. Mick stayed in our room.

I had been in bed less than ten minutes when the phone rang. It was Mick. "Honey," he said, "come back here and sleep with me."

I raced down the hallway and we spent the night in each other's arms. That is the insanity of alcohol, right there, in a Kodak moment. But the next morning, when he sobered up, Mick could hardly look at me. I guess we both knew it was ending. We had gone into counseling. The therapist told me then we ought to separate. He said, "Mickey is totally controlled by fear. He is filled with fear about everything."

Even then, no one really knew what I was going through. I don't think the boys knew how humiliated I felt, how much despair I felt.

For one thing, when I wasn't bopping him on the head, I covered it up so well. When we took trips, we still looked great together. I could get all dressed up and drink all I wanted and people would be nice to me because I was Mickey Mantle's wife. I had no identity of my own. Just his.

But I loved him, and I would still catch a glimpse now and then of the boy in the football jacket. These sightings came on days when his behavior wasn't controlled by his drinking.

This was the dizzy path we plodded down in the late eighties. The memorabilia craze had taken his fame to a new crest. People were paying $110,000 at auctions for an old Mantle jersey. He was a hero all over again. He had renewed in fans a sense of the past. Meanwhile, our family was falling apart.

We were spending a quiet day in January of 1988, talking calmly and with some politeness. Then, with just enough energy to get the sentence out, he said, "I'm leaving." I watched him pack and make several trips to the car. Finally, I started to help him carry his things outside and put them in the trunk. I looked at him and said, "What are you doing, Mick? Do you know what you're doing?"

He said, "You will always be my wife. I know I'm giving up the best thing I ever had."

I said, "I don't even understand what you're talking about. What do you mean? I will always be your wife, but you don't want a life with me?"

He didn't say another word. He drove off and I went back inside the house, vowing that he would never see me cry. He came back later that day, maybe to see how I was, maybe to pick up something he had overlooked. While he was there, the new woman in his life called. She said, "I really love Mickey." And I said, "Well, I love him, too." That was the only real conversation I had with her. She called our house in Joplin after his mother died, and was startled to find that I was with him. She was ugly and snarly with me on the phone. She probably thought he was cheating on her with his wife.

For a time that now seems short to me, but may have gone on for months, our separation was nasty. There was a lot of bickering over petty things, and when Mick came to town and invited me to dinner with the boys, I refused. They always told me he was disappointed and knowing Mick, I believe he was.

The boys also told me that Dad was afraid of me. I hadn't imagined that. They said he was fearful that I might go off the deep end and try to kill him. I thought about it. He must have felt he had given me plenty of cause.

But my focus right then was trying to figure out how to get through the day. The minute my eyes flew open in the morning, I felt like my hair was standing on end. I was so used to planning my day for Mick. My life was a mess. All I could think was, What the hell am I going to do?

I really did try to drown my sorrow in a bottle. It was odd. I never liked the taste of alcohol, and never found a drink I really liked. But I kept trying. Eventually, somebody asked me, "Have you ever tried vodka and soda with a twist of lime?" I did, and that became my drink of choice. I could put away a lot of vodka because it had no aroma or taste. I even had my own favorite brand, Finlandia. I enjoyed getting drunk. It made me forget. When I went out, it was with the boys. They were great at looking after me. But I did a lot of my drinking at home, by myself.

After we had been separated three months, he called one night, drunk and sobbing. He was in town and he wanted to come back. He wanted to be together again. He told me he had caught his lady friend fooling around with another guy, a friend of Billy Martin's. I'm sure she did it to make him jealous. My mistake was letting him come home. He stayed three weeks and then took off again, leaving me even more angry and depressed.

After six months, I had still not sought any help for myself. No counseling. Nothing. I would just drink until I fell asleep.

One night, a friend called while I was crying and having

a fit. What I was saying frightened her, and when we hung up my phone started ringing. I talked to the first caller nearly an hour, a lady who had been in Alcoholics Anonymous. She must have evaluated my case because a second woman called who had been through a self-help program for the families of alcoholics.

It helped to have someone listen. She was the one who told me Mick's womanizing was part of the disease. I had never thought of it that way. Of course, I had never thought of him as being an alcoholic.

She invited me to a meeting the next night. If she had not gone with me, I might not have gone back because the whole idea was intimidating. But I did, and I kept going back. I dived into the literature. I felt like every page in every book they had was written for me. I was there every time the door opened. I was hungry. I couldn't get enough of it. There was no doubt in my mind that God put me there. That in itself was quite a turnaround. When I went that first night, my attitude was, I don't want to hear anything about God. I mean, that just turned me off instantly because God had been out of my life for so long.

I went during the day and at night. Sometimes I went to three meetings a day. I continued to drink, although not as much. If I was with someone who was drinking, I drank, because in my mind I still didn't have a problem. Everybody else had one. But not me.

After going to the meetings for about three months, I sought out a sponsor, the one I still have today. She was what they call a black belt in the program. Tough. An earth mother with long black hair and no pretenses. She had been in the program for thirty years. When I called her, she asked, "Do you really want this? Do you really want to work at it? Because if not, I have no interest in sponsoring you. I want people who really want to work at the program."

My recovery was just beginning. But I had taken a big step for a nervous lady. The healing has been slow for me because I was fifty-six when I got into the program. Most people seek help at an earlier age. My sponsor still reminds me of how I looked that first night: "You had a wild look on your face. Your eyes were as big as dinner plates. You were looking around like a cornered animal."

My mind was in disarray, but as strange as it may sound, I felt at home. I didn't have any concern that I was going to be on display because I was the wife of Mickey Mantle. That was one of the best parts about the program. No last names. I was just Merlyn. Unless you're famous yourself, no one is likely to know or recognize you. Only my sponsor knew who I was.

When some people hear references to a twelve-step program, I'm sure they think of Al Franken's character, Stuart Smalley, on *Saturday Night Live.* He's the one who looks in a mirror and says, "I'm good enough, I'm smart enough and, doggone it, people like me." But the bottom line is, the program works.

I went with my sponsor to a conference in Florida, where I got to hear the alcoholics tell their stories of strength and hope. It was a huge boost for me. I just fell in love with all of that; I could relate to so much that was said.

As a bonus, our son David had moved to Florida to take a job. He came over and visited with me while I was there.

I was talking to Mickey by then, but we were still on a

seesaw. One time he would call and be sweet and tender and worried about the boys. He loved them, but didn't know how to show it. He was too much of a kid himself. The next time he would be drunk and hostile and saying things to upset me, I thought, in order to please the lady standing listening to his end of the call.

When we had our quiet talks, Mick always said, "I don't want a divorce, but you can have one if you want it." I didn't, but at some point my anger boiled over again and I thought about it. I hired an attorney, and after I did Mick had my phone tapped. It was just another weird twist in the rope that bound us. I never suspected at the time that he had recorded my calls and was listening to them.

He told me later that he just wanted to hear what everyone said about him, and I think that was the truth. In any case, he got an earful. We were all mad at him, including the boys. During one conversation with a friend, he heard me refer to him as "a drunken sonofabitch."

Now that made him mad. When he tried to tell Roy True what I had said, Roy threw up his hands: "Don't tell me anything. I don't want to hear anything you've heard. It's illegal and you can't use any of it in court, regardless." Mick had hired a former FBI guy and the tap went on for about a month. I always thought Mick felt so guilty, he needed to know what we were saying about him.

For the first time, I couldn't go to Roy with my troubles. He was there to protect Mick. But he is simply too decent a man to let me make a huge mistake. He said to me, off the record, "Merlyn, don't get a divorce. Mick doesn't want one." Later, he told me, "It's going to be much better because you waited this out."

He was right, of course. He usually was. Mick was doing well with the card shows and his other contracts, but in the early nineties he was pulling in serious money. When we first talked about a living allowance, I just pulled a figure out of the air. Let's just say it was around the figure the Yankees were paying Mick in his last years.

On behalf of his client, Roy said, "That's outlandish. He can't afford that." I said, "I don't care. If we don't get a divorce, that's what I want." Eventually, I got it.

But our separation was never about money. It was about making compromises. If he had been just a drunk, but a faithful drunk, I would have put up with it. I had put up with all the looniness for thirty-six years, when he walked out the first time. I even tried to match him drink for drink, and that was my downfall. That just fed the monster; my anger turned to rage. We would sit there drinking for hours until a fight started. It could be about anything. Most of the time it was about the things he had done that hurt me.

My sponsor said that as long as I let Mick come and go in my life, I was not going to stop feeling as I did. But I could never let go. I could not let go of my home. I could not let go of my marriage. I could not let go of my husband. In time, things were good again and the push came in an unexpected way.

It started not with me, but Danny, who was always there for everybody. The other boys were wonderful to me. But David lived in Florida for a couple of years. And Mickey Jr. was so hurt about his dad he sort of faded into the scenery. Billy was into his drugs and alcohol, unable to take care of himself, much less lend support to anyone else. Billy became my project.

Danny could be a moderator because he lived with Mick—or maybe it was the other way around. Right after the separation, I was always going to Danny for information, which was so unfair. After I began to get into recovery, I backed off and left Mick alone. It came just in time. I was either going to drink myself to death or wind up as a traffic statistic. The program saved my life.

It was Danny who checked himself into the Betty Ford Center in late 1993, and Kay, his wife-to-be, soon joined him. I went out to visit them during family week.

Not all of my pain had vanished, but most of it had. I was comfortable now, living my life the way I wanted. That was how I accepted the way we were. I still hadn't cut myself off from the bottle. I hadn't made up my mind about making that commitment.

On the Fourth of July, a few months before I finally stopped, I went home to Oklahoma to have a birthday party for my mother. The air-conditioning wasn't working in the house, and nothing went right. We wound up having a rotten meal at a restaurant. I was exhausted and disappointed that I had not been able to throw a party for her.

Driving back to Dallas, I kept thinking, "I wish I had a drink." I couldn't get it out of my head. So I stopped in MacAllister at the Holiday Inn, checked into a room, and went to the bar. I got sloshed. I began to notice that this sort of thing was still happening. If I was in our house in Joplin and there was no one else around, I would take a bottle of wine and sit outside and watch the golfers until the sun went down and it began to get cold. I enjoyed drinking by myself. I didn't need a crowd.

I'm not sure anyone knew what a delicate time it was

for me. They knew I was in a program and they were glad. Mom had found something that kept her busy and took her mind off Dad. That was how they saw my recovery.

Mick and I began to have a good and caring relationship again. I don't know if he paid any attention to what I was doing, or observed any change in me. He was still drunk most of the time. Like the kids, I think he was relieved that I had gotten off his back. I began to get some peace inside. We could go out together and not have this thick tension between us, or any name-calling. I did that; Mick never called me names.

I was following one course for recovery, yet I was still in my old behavior. I had cut back to the extent that I was now spending more time around people who didn't drink. But when Mick came to town, we would go to dinner and I'd have two or three drinks. When I was with my sons and the waiter asked if he could bring us anything, my first instinct was to order a vodka tonic. I drank less, but with more guilt.

On the plane going to Palm Springs to visit Danny, I had a drink so I could better monitor the engines. But I abstained the whole time I was there. I had called a friend who lived out there, who had been in my high school class and was a recovering alcoholic. When I got ready to go home, Bud and the kids came to the airport to see me off.

While I waited to board the plane, I ordered a very stiff vodka in the bar. Bud raised an eyebrow and said, "Do you think you should be doing that in front of Danny and Kay?" I said, "Oh, sure. It's all right. They know I'm afraid of flying."

When the plane took off, I settled back in my seat. I

started to think about what he had said. I told myself, "You selfish, selfish witch. Here you are so happy that your child got sober, and here you are still drinking."

That became my sobriety date—November 2, 1993. I knew at that moment it was going to be the last time I had a drink. I haven't really wanted one. I haven't needed one.

Now there was a domino effect. When Danny and Kay came home, they didn't preach to him, but Mick was curious about every minute they spent, every test and exercise they had. In January, Mick amazed us all. He not only went to the Betty Ford Center and got sober, he announced that he had gone and exposed himself to the intense scrutiny that Americans save for their fallen angels.

David was the next to go, and Mickey Jr. was pondering. We were all in various stages of recovery. We all began to feel that we had a common bond, a fellowship of survival. Four of us (including Kay) had stopped drinking in a three-month period. We had adopted a new discipline and stayed with it. We had reached out to one another and made a new connection.

There was one shadow across the morning sun, one that we were expecting. We could do nothing to save Billy.

Chapter 5

Billy

NOT QUITE TWO YEARS AFTER BILLY DIED, I RECEIVED a call from a man at the mortuary, telling me a letter had been delivered there addressed to Billy Mantle. I said I would drive over to pick it up.

I assumed the mail was from one of his drug friends, someone who was trying to get into recovery. Or they might have wanted help or money from Billy's family.

The letter was from a girl. She said, "I've thought of you every day since your death. How kind you were to me, when no one else was." That was all. It was sweet and sad and touching. She asked nothing. She was simply thanking Billy for caring.

The return address on the envelope was from the women's prison in Gatesville, Texas. She was trying to get her life straightened out.

I cry just thinking about the letter and what it meant.

For two or three years before Mick's death, I kept so much of my feeling inside that I couldn't cry. Now I can't seem to stop.

Not a day goes by that I don't wonder what we might have done that would have made Billy's life better. I thought of the girl, and how close he had come to winding up where she was. He was high on drugs one night, and walked around his apartment firing a gun. He nearly shot a man in the swimming pool. He was nuts about guns, and this one got him into the most serious of his many scrapes. I can't think of a creepier combination than someone on drugs waving a gun.

I had people tell me, "Well, maybe some time behind bars would do him good, get Billy to turn himself around." I heard the stories from friends of mine in the program who had served time. I was afraid he would get into fights and someone would kill him. We hired a very good attorney and he was given probation.

This goes against everything the professionals tell you about dependency: Don't bail them out of trouble. But that was one rule I could not observe. I may have done Billy more harm than good because I was definitely his enabler. I would have done anything to keep my son out of jail. Help him or not, it wasn't going to cure his cancer.

In 1977, Billy woke up one morning with a lump in the lymph node under his ear. The lump was removed the same day and we waited for the results to come back from the lab.

It was not until later that I learned that Billy had been given the test results—the lump was malignant. He had Hodgkin's disease. But the doctor asked him not to say anything. Mick was out of town and the doctor said he wanted to inform the two of us at the same time.

So our nineteen-year-old son kept this frightful information to himself for that night and part of the next day. I sensed something when I saw Billy not long after he came out from under the anesthetic. His attitude changed immediately. He was irritated and abrasive. He had taken on a strange new personality. And why not? He felt the bitterness any nineteen-year-old might feel after being told his future had been stolen from him. When Mick arrived, the doctor broke the news to us. We were crushed. He said they would start him on chemotherapy right away.

After a few months, the disease went into remission. But Billy felt he was doomed, and this attitude invaded our whole family. The boys had grown up with the stories of Hodgkin's and the Mantle men. I feared for Mick as he neared forty, but frankly I never thought the disease would reach out and snare one of my children.

In a general way, I always worried more about Billy. There is a Billy in most families, always the underdog, the one who has to run the obstacle course. He was born with dyslexia, a reading disability, getting letters and numbers reversed. We enrolled him in a private school in Dallas, as we had all our boys. At the Lamplighter's School, special teachers gave him remedial help.

Billy was wound a little tighter than the other boys, but he had the softest heart. He was the kind who would carry a bug to the door and release it rather than kill it.

After Billy was diagnosed, Mickey turned even more inward and retreated into a shell of his own guilt. But Billy rallied. He went to work in the oil fields, drove a big truck, and loved the job. He liked getting dirty and sweaty under the Texas sun, working with men who were old hands at exploring the earth and its riches.

Then one day in 1981, he got sick on the job, and came home to be reexamined. The symptoms were the same and, of course, the Hodgkin's was active again. He underwent another six months of chemotherapy, and new tests showed that the cancer had spread. It had jumped from the lymph nodes to his liver and bone marrow.

I made up my mind to take him to the M. D. Anderson Cancer Center in Houston, where many of the newest cancer treatments had been developed. Mick agreed. We drove down with Billy stretched out in the back seat, squirming to get comfortable. In Houston, they did another battery of tests. The doctor, a kind and sympathetic man, invited us into his office. "We don't lie to people here," he said. "Billy has a twenty-five percent chance of surviving this."

Then he told us about an experimental program they had just started on the first group of patients. We signed the forms the hospital required, enrolling Billy in the program. As I look back, the worst part was that we didn't think to give him a choice. We didn't say, "This is your body. Do you want to do this?" It didn't occur to us. We just wanted him to get well. We didn't want him to die.

The doctors started the experimental chemo. After the first treatment, he was so sick he vomited all night, and woke up every patient on the floor. Over the next few weeks, he seemed to deteriorate before my eyes. He lost every hair on his body. Gradually, he began to improve. We went home to Dallas, and he came back to Houston for treatments three or four days at a time. They would hook him to the tubes, and pour the chemicals into him.

In Dallas, he was getting another kind of treatment every two weeks. This schedule went on for six months. When he wasn't connected to a machine, Billy went to a fitness center and worked out with weights. He began to rebuild his body. His hair grew back; how degraded he had felt, a young boy, nineteen, wanting to date, looking emaciated and bald.

When we went to his doctor's office in Dallas for his biannual checkup, the nurses couldn't believe he was the same person. He looked muscular, his skin tone was good, his hair had grown back. We were so proud of Billy. He was in remission again.

In the meantime, we were unaware that he had gotten hooked on the painkiller Dilaudid. He had a prescription for the pills in both Dallas and Houston, and he kept finding ways to refill them. I learned later that the street value of Dilaudid was $40 or $50 a pill.

Our denial was so great about our own problems, how could we have recognized his? We found out about Billy's addiction when Mick walked into the trophy room one day and found him grinding the pills into powder. He still had the catheter in his chest for the chemo. He would mix the powder with a little water, and with a syringe inject it into the catheter.

Mick was beside himself. He had a fairly loose attitude about what was moral, but he detested the idea of drugs: the use of needles, the scum who peddled it, the whole culture. It was evil. It was unlawful. It was a weakness. And now he knew it had penetrated his family.

We checked Billy into a psychiatric hospital for the first time for treatment. It seemed as if half the patients in the hospital had been friends of his at Hillcrest High School. He completed the program, but the doctors wanted him to stay longer. Mick said no—Billy had begged his dad to get him out—and we took him home. The doctors warned us that Billy was mentally disturbed and possibly suicidal. He had never made any threats of that kind and we were defensive about how much he had already endured.

His drug use got worse, and so did his drinking, and he went from speed to crack. He started to hang out with the most sordid-looking street people. When we saw him with some of his new friends, we were afraid for him. But Billy was in his own world. He thought a kind heart would always protect him. He told me how he brought food one night to a man who was homeless and hungry, who then threw it into a trash can. Billy walked away, hurt and confused.

Billy was a giving person, even when he was all mixed up on drugs. If someone else needed it, he would give away the last dollar he had.

The years went by and I made the trips to Houston with Billy, checked him in and out of rehab, and kept house for him when he wasn't disappearing for days or weeks at a time. I made the final, wrenching decision to move in part because of Billy. It was just the two of us in the house in Preston Hollow, and frequently it was just me.

I reached a point where I was afraid to be there. The house had been broken into and robbed a couple of times. Once I walked in and the thieves were still in the house.

I suspected that they were drug friends of Billy's who knew where he lived and figured the house would be easy pickings. When I drove into the garage that night, I didn't even notice that it was dark on the patio. They had unscrewed all the lights in the back of the house and had disconnected the burglar alarm.

As I came in the front door, I heard them scurry out the back. They hadn't yet started to burglarize the house. They had taken the pillow cases off the pillows and were getting ready to fill them up. They were looking, I imagine, for jewelry and silver and cash. There was a small gun in the drawer by the bedside, which they found and tossed into a chair. One of them had tested the trigger and the gun had jammed. I couldn't help but think, If they had gotten it to work, would they have been less quick to leave? Would they have killed me?

The neighborhood was still pretty, but it was hard to feel secure when you knew Billy was hanging out with some unsavory types. He was not oblivious to that fact, either. He worried about keeping an eye out for his family. He nearly always had a gun on him or close by. I don't know if he was paranoid, or if he had good reasons to arm himself.

It was traumatic for me to move out of a home I had lived in for thirty-six years. I bought a condominium in an exclusive high-rise building in another part of town. It was hurtful to leave a home I loved, with majestic trees and so many memories. I was surprised to find out later how much the boys hated that house. I asked each of them to house-sit for a few days during my move. Each tried to beg off. To them it had not been a happy place. What they remembered was the tension and ugly scenes and bad vibrations. I didn't realize they felt that way.

I still drive by there from time to time. A young couple with small children bought the house, and I'm curious about the alterations they might make. We had paid $59,500 for it in 1958, right after Mick's career had blossomed. All those years later, we sold it for $450,000, which tells us something about inflation, and how the times have changed.

We bought Billy a small condo in a complex a block away from mine. I had reached a point where I didn't want him living with me, doing drugs. I thought Billy would be better off having his own place, not being under his mother's wing.

I had not yet moved to the high-rise, and Billy was still in the house. He was hyper, insisting that I take him to a couple of doctors. He wasn't feeling well, but by then he seldom did. I thought he just wanted me to take him on his rounds, until he found a doctor who would write another prescription.

As he went on and on, I was having trouble breathing. When I woke up that morning, everything caught up with me. The transition to living alone was hard. Disposing of the contents of my home, and furnishing the new one, left me drained.

I was having a heart attack. The pain seemed to be not so much in my chest as in my back. Billy could see I was having cold sweats. He pulled himself together and called an ambulance. Before the paramedics lifted me onto a stretcher, they gave me a nitroglycerin capsule. They gave me another on the way to the hospital, put an oxygen mask over my face, and started me on the IV fluids. Billy followed us in my car.

After they checked me in, my own physician examined

me and told me I was going to need heart surgery. I asked Billy to call the other boys so they would know where we were. When one of them called back—I think it was Danny—I told him that Billy had my car. Even in the valley of the shadow, I had to worry that Billy might just take off, or hock my car.

The boys called Mick home from California, where he was traveling with David for Upper Deck. He returned and the next day I was under the knife. I was really very lucky. We had reached the hospital quickly enough to limit the damage to my heart. I had two clogged arteries, and the operation, a double bypass, went smoothly. When I came out of surgery, still under the anesthesia, I was thrashing, clawing at the tube in my throat. The boys told me later that Mick broke down and started sobbing.

He brought me flowers every day, but he never stayed more than a few minutes. Mick ran from hospital rooms, from any kind of sickness. He made a point of telling the boys, "I want you to know I love your mother. And I want you guys to look after her."

The only one I hadn't seen, since the day I entered the hospital, was Billy. I had a strange foreboding. No one had seen him for days. No one could find him. Then one day a call came to my room from the office of another hospital. Billy had checked himself in, and a week after my operation, he had one of his own. A team of surgeons sort of glued his heart back together. He had a bypass and two valves replaced. While he was on the operating table, he suffered a stroke that left him paralyzed on one side. He dragged one of his legs when he walked, but he had pulled through. Billy was like a cat with nine lives.

We came home from the hospital, back to the house in Preston Hollow, a day or two apart. We both had nurses with us in our separate bedrooms. One day Billy overdosed on some kind of medication and began bleeding from the nose and mouth. I began to have chest pains again. By now I felt I had no other choice. I asked the nurses to take Billy back to the hospital. I couldn't lie there and try to get well and watch my son try to kill himself in the next room.

An ambulance took Billy back to the hospital. After he was gone, a maid straightened up his bed and found the pills tucked between the sheet and the mattress. He had kept a supply on hand to use in addition to what the nurses were giving him.

After a few days his condition was stable. When he was released, he moved into his own apartment. A few more weeks passed before I was strong enough to move into mine.

The doctors told him he could no longer abuse drugs or drink or smoke and, of course, he went right back to all three.

All of us hauled around our own guilt about Billy. We all stayed on his case about what he was doing to himself, but at the same time we were all drinking, and the boys were going through their own drug phases.

Still, no matter how many times Billy went into rehab, nothing stuck. No one could talk to him.

Once he was suspended from school. Billy Martin was managing the Texas Rangers, and Mick and the boys thought he might listen to his godfather. No one gave a better pep talk, or a reality check, than Billy Martin.

Mick's father,
Elvin (Mutt) Mantle,
groomed his son for
the big leagues from
the age of four.

At fifteen, Mickey Jr.
looks sharp in his military
school uniform.

All photographs courtesy of the Mantle family.

He was not yet "the Mick," Merlyn was not yet a blonde,
but the innocence of 1951 made those the best of times.

You could see the effort, and sometimes the pain, as a grimacing Mick literally swings from the heels.

Merlyn and Mick leave Yankee Stadium for a night
on the town in 1965.

Four-year-old Danny
plays peekaboo over
Mom's shoulder.

OPPOSITE: Posing right-handed, the switch-hitting
Mickey Mantle had the home run slugger's form.

Joan Ford and Merlyn Mantle are all smiles on the day in 1974 that pals Whitey and Mick were inducted into the Hall of Fame.

The two Mickeys take a break: Junior was catching that day,
Senior was grabbing some shade.

David, wearing familiar Number 7, swings
for the fence in a Fantasy Camp game.

Mallory gives dad, Mickey Jr., a warm embrace.

Danny and Kay with their godson in 1990, practicing for a baby to be named later.

Mick has a firm grip on Mallory, who is suited up and ready to play.

Merlyn has a hug for her
granddaughters:
Mallory and Marilyn.

In this house they never ran out
of M&Ms. Grandma and Grandad
enjoy cuddling with Marilyn,
David and Marla's "little princess."

Christmas 1992 (from left): Kay; Cindy; Mallory; Mickey Jr.;
Danny; Billy; David; Marla; Mickey Sr.;
Merlyn's mom, Reba; and Merlyn.

A Mantle family Christmas (from left): Mickey Sr., David,
Danny, Marilyn, Mallory, Marla, and Kay, in 1994.

Merlyn and Mick celebrate their forty-third wedding
anniversary in December 1994.

Take a guess: Is that a Christmas sweater
Mick is wearing on December 25, 1994?

With fountain pens lined up,
Mick is set for some
heavy autograph signing.

Mickey Sr. and Danny pay one of their last visits to
Lovell Mantle, Mick's mother and the matriarch of the clan.

Mick poses in front of one of his boyhood homes.

Where he got his start, in Commerce, Oklahoma, the street of dreams that is now Mickey Mantle Boulevard.

It was an extra-special day when Danny and Kay were married. A few eyes may have been wet, but the wedding party was dry.

Danny and Kay with Will, in December 1995; Mickey Sr. didn't live to see his first grandson.

Here come the Mantles—Mickey Jr., Mickey Sr., David, and
Danny at their last Fantasy Camp together, in 1994.

The Mantle brothers stick together: Mickey Jr., David,
and Danny helped coach the Fantasy Campers in '94.

The whole team was on hand for this camp:
David, the two Mickeys, Billy, and Danny.

The only problem was, when he got to the house after that night's ball game, Billy Martin was so drunk he was tongue-tied. Mick watched his old teammate rant and rave, and then he turned to young Billy and asked, "Do you understand what he's saying?"

Billy said, "No, I don't have any idea."

Then Mick turned to Danny and David and said, "Hell, neither do I." At that point, the two Yankee drinking buddies nearly got into a fight. When they left, Mick insisted that Billy Martin leave the house first because he thought his old friend might hit him from behind.

Our Billy took the scene right in stride. From the day he found out about his illness, he was a loner. He didn't let many people get close to him, and he would often pull away if anyone tried to give him a hug. We can only guess what a young man goes through when he's nineteen and may die at any time.

The disease went into remission three times, but all the while he was wearing out his heart. I try not to think about how he died, and where. He had been arrested for driving while intoxicated, and was locked up in a minimum security jail. During the night, he complained of chest pains. In the morning, a Saturday, the police moved him to Parkland General Hospital.

At noon, they were walking him to lunch when he suddenly clutched his chest and fell to the ground. By the time they got him back to the emergency room and a doctor examined him, it was too late.

The medical examiner called the house. David and his wife, Marla, were staying there while we tried to sell it. David called Danny, who drove to Preston Trail to tell

Mick. When Danny saw him, he had just gotten out of the shower. He had a towel wrapped around him and a glass of water in his hand. He took one look at Danny's face, saw the tears on his cheeks, and put the glass down.

The three of them, Danny, Kay, and Mick, went over to the condo and waited for me to get home. It was Mick who told me. He said, "Merlyn, it's Billy. He's dead."

I lost it completely. Mick caught me and held me and I cried great wracking sobs for the adorable boy who had so many hills he couldn't quite climb. Mick stayed with me that night in March 1994. We slept in the same bed, but that was the last night Mick spent with me. My mother came down from Oklahoma and stayed with me for a few days.

That was a testing time for Mickey. I really wanted and needed him to be with me. Losing a child is really the ultimate loss. I felt so much guilt about Billy, so much anger about the vagaries of life and death. But Mick had been sober only three months and he couldn't feel anything. He was just trying to get through it.

The day we made the arrangements for the funeral service, he was late getting to the mortuary. When he threw open the door, he had a stricken look on his face. But I didn't worry about him taking a drink. Anyone who understood Mickey Mantle knew that he had made a deal. If he had to spend the rest of his life in a wine cellar, he would have stayed sober, because he had given his word. That was the way he was.

What worried me was how he would handle the reality of Billy's life. The boys and I wanted to have a visitation for his friends the night before the burial. Mick flatly refused.

In his mind, Billy's friends were the ones he shared drugs with, or the long-haired, shabby, unclean, and sometimes demented strangers he met on the streets.

A little article appeared in the Dallas newspaper, just two or three short paragraphs, and he wasn't happy with that. He wanted only the family at the funeral, no guests. We did it the way Dad wanted it.

Later, I was mad at myself because I knew we were wrong. I told the boys, "You know, we should have had something for Billy's friends, whoever they were. That was Billy's good-bye, not Dad's. We should have let his friends come and pay their respects. If Mick didn't want to be there when they did, he didn't have to be there."

We did our grieving for Billy separately. But my relationship with Mick improved. We would not put this particular sadness behind us, but we had turned a new page in our lives.

When I first went into my program, I was instructed to always tell Mick that I loved him. Alcoholics—and I should have had an instinct for this on my own—usually feel unloved. When I talked to Mick on the phone, or we said good night at the door after dinner, I always told him, "Mick, I love you." He always gave me a hug and said, "I love you, too."

The obvious question is, If this was true, then why were we no longer living together? I don't have a glib answer. Why was Billy the one who had to get Hodgkin's?

A few weeks after the funeral, Danny and Kay were married, a happy occasion that I think was unspoiled by Billy's absence. In a way, his brothers felt some relief because his misery and pain were over and he had not died a violent death. We all had waited for years, wondering if a call would come in the night telling us that Billy had been shot or stabbed.

Looking back, I marvel at Billy's toughness. In spite of his addictions, he lived for seventeen years with a cancer that had spread across his body, and with a weak and ailing heart. He smoked, he drank, he popped pills. He never stopped caring about people who could do nothing for him.

In the end, the cancer couldn't kill him. His heart gave out. There has to be a victory in all of this, somewhere.

Part Three

The Brothers

... many of them miss the point. The most repeated story about Dad and me involves the first time I went to a bar and tasted my first beer. It wouldn't be worth telling, except that I was three years old.

—*MICKEY JR.*

When you go into treatment, they tell you each child has a different role. I was the clown, the one who wants to make everybody laugh. ... For most of his life, Mickey Mantle landed on his feet. I was the one who kept landing on his head.

—*DAVID*

The only game I actually remember seeing him play in, he hit home runs back to back. ... I saw him run around the bases, heard the crowd screaming his name. ... Even then I knew he was famous. ... His kind of famous caused people to imagine they were him in their dreams.

—*DANNY*

Chapter 6

Mickey Jr.

Mickey Jr. was born in April 1953, just in time for opening day. In June, I flew with him to New York so he could finally meet his daddy. My sister, Pat, was with us. Mick was waiting at the airport with Billy Martin.

I handed him little Mick and he didn't say a word. He had an expression on his face that was close to awe. He cradled him in his arms and looked at him. He just kept looking at him. There was something else in his eyes, a question. I always thought he was wondering, "Am I ready for this? Am I ready to be a father?"

—MERLYN

ONE CHRISTMAS EVE, I WAS RIDING AROUND WITH Dad, running errands, and he pulled into a filling station for gas. When we walked inside to pay, we saw a middle-aged black man standing at the counter, close to tears. He had a battered old car with a flat tire, and the back seat was piled high with presents.

The guy who ran the gas station was ignoring him.

He had the look of a man who had been saving all year to afford those presents. Dad asked him if he needed any help. He said he didn't have a spare. If he couldn't get the tire fixed he had no way to get home to put the gifts under the tree.

When Dad called the attendant over, it was as if his voice had just yanked him by the shirt. He slapped three one-hundred-dollar bills on the counter and said, "Put two new tires on this man's car. Do it now, right now, dammit, so he can get home and give his kids their Christmas presents."

I don't know if the man knew his Good Samaritan was Mickey Mantle or not. Dad had been out of baseball for a couple of years. It wasn't just the season, or the spot the man was in, that moved him. He didn't like seeing someone's pride get trampled.

Some people give millions and have buildings named after them. His were small acts of charity, but he did them all the time. He always handed some cash to the guys who panhandled on street corners. He was on a first-name basis with one guy. He gave him money every time he passed that corner. He was always there and he always gave him a sort of half-salute and said, "Thanks, Mick."

He taught us kindness, and taught us by example, not to boast about it or expect anything in return. I think those were good things to teach your kids.

What he didn't do was teach us how to drink. We learned that on our own, by the time we were in high school. It's true he didn't discourage us, and as we grew older he made room for us at the bar. But that was the way real men partied, and we all wanted to be real men. Those were years of ignorance, society's as well as his and ours. We could have stopped tagging along anytime we wanted.

It was Mickey Mantle who kept saying what an awful dad he was, not his sons. I thought he was a great dad. We would go months without seeing him, but we understood: that was because of his job. He left home to play baseball in February and he didn't return until mid-October, or later, because the Yankees were nearly always in the World Series. When he came home, the last thing he wanted to do was play ball in the back yard, the way his father had. But Mutt Mantle worked 400 feet below the ground. Baseball wasn't a job to him, it was an escape. Even after Dad retired, he still made much of his money on the road.

It wasn't as if he ignored us. He called nearly every day, from wherever he was. He was always a good listener. He would give you an opinion if you asked for one. But when we were old enough to need advice, he felt his own mistakes disqualified him from volunteering any.

No, he wasn't what you would call a regular dad. But then, he didn't lead what you would call a regular life.

I have to admit that I had an advantage over my brothers. I'm the lucky one, the firstborn son, the one who had a chance to see him in his prime, and be around him before the heavy drinking took over.

The fact that I took up golf when I was seven, and we had that as a common interest, gave us a way of spending time together. But more than golf, our family and friends all say I'm the one who was most like him. And I was: stubborn and hardheaded. I hope I inherited a quality or two from the other side of him, the side that would stand up for a friend against the entire Chinese army.

I want to be careful not to sound like I'm making excuses for him. You had to accept him the way he was, as a great ballplayer, and a bashful, purehearted person, probably the least calculating human being you could ever meet. He didn't like to hear excuses made for him when he was alive, and he doesn't need any in death.

I don't know if they keep records in this area, but I suspect that if you're born with a famous name the results tend to balance out. Half the time was fun and half the time being Mickey Mantle Jr. was a burden. When I was younger, I considered the name a nuisance. Today, it's an asset. In my sales work for a chemical company, my business card gets me in the door fairly quickly.

I wouldn't take anything for the things I experienced with my father, the good, the bad, and the dumb. Some of the stories have been given different interpretations, and many of them miss the point.

The most repeated story about Dad and me involves the first time I went to a bar and tasted my first beer. It wouldn't be worth telling, except that I was three years old. Believe it or not, the memory is my own and I can still recall it clearly.

This was the winter after my dad's Triple Crown year in 1956, another Christmas. He was babysitting me that day and he took me with him to a bar called Mendenhall's, right on Main Street in Commerce, where you followed the curve of the road if you were driving to Miami, Oklahoma.

I was sitting on the bar with a beer in my hand. I'm sure it was my dad's. He would not have bought me a bottle, and he didn't need this one at the moment because he was rolling around on the floor, fighting a guy. He got into it taking up for the bartender, who had tried to calm down a drunk and unruly customer.

In the middle of the fight, while I was sitting there, watching, my grandfather, Giles Johnson, came in the door. He was a small man, but wiry and with a no-nonsense nature. He scooped me off the bar with both arms and, on his way out, he walked by my dad and kicked him in the side of the head. "Don't ever let me catch you with this kid in here again," he said.

That night I slept at my grandparents' home. Dad didn't say much when he picked me up the next morning, but I know he hated to face Grandpa Johnson.

He didn't think there was anything immoral about taking me to the bar. He wanted to show me off, and this was where he was most likely to bump into his friends.

He was very much a product of his times. You looked for a ticket to a bigger town or a better life, or you scratched out a living the way your daddy did before you. Happiness was having two parents, a car with good wheels, and marrying the first girl you ever loved.

He was twenty when he married Mom, a father at twenty-two, the father of four sons before he was twenty-eight. (I didn't marry until I turned thirty-five.) By the time we were teenagers, he treated us as his equals, meaning that he treated us like kids. He was as big a kid as any of us. I've always said my mom raised five boys.

But that was part of what made him Mickey Mantle. By the time I was seven, I already knew how hard it was going to be to spend any quality time with him. And not because he didn't try. He took me to a driving range to hit a few buckets of golf balls. I don't think we finished the first bucket. This was supposed to be our time together. It ended up with him being mobbed. They kept interrupting him, wanting an autograph or just to talk to him.

As I got older, I learned to accept this because I had no choice. All during my school years, other kids wanted to meet him, and even their parents. I tried to put it off when I could because he was never comfortable with that type of attention. I probably knew less about his baseball records than they did. I never followed him as a star player because I never saw him act that way. He was just Dad to me.

The upside came during those summers when school let out, and we moved to New Jersey for the balance of the baseball season. First it was just me, then David, Billy, and Danny. We may have missed a game or two at Yankee Stadium, but not many. We would hang out with Yogi Berra's kids and Whitey Ford's kids. The front office put aside seats for us in the stands, but we didn't spend much time sitting in them.

We didn't watch much of the games, either, but I saw him hit three home runs in a doubleheader, two left-handed and one right-handed, against the Senators. That was awesome, even to an eight- or nine-year-old. One of them landed in the thirty-second, and last, row of the bleachers. It was the tenth time in the history of baseball a hitter had homered from both sides of the plate—and dad was responsible for nine of them.

The crowd went bananas that day, but I had learned not to trust the temper of a crowd. New York fans could be mean and nasty, and I never understood it when they turned on him, when they booed and heckled him. I didn't like it and when the anger came I would often take refuge down in the clubhouse.

Dad didn't like us to be running loose in there when the players were around. But they had a television room just off the main area, and we would watch TV until the players had gone to the field. Then we could do whatever we wanted.

When the players were at their lockers, that was their space. Casey Stengel didn't want us getting in the way, and he wouldn't put up with much horseplay, but he was always great with kids. In all the years I went to the stadium, I don't remember a player who was mean to us. There was one coach we were always told to stay away from and that was Frank Crosetti. He was a little crabby, but mostly he didn't like noise and for a kid that was like taking away the air.

There was a story about the old Yankees, and how Crosetti, Tony Lazzeri, and Joe DiMaggio always sat in the hotel lobby together, just watching whatever was going on, not talking for hours at a time. They may have been the three quietest Italians ever to play on the same club.

One day, a writer, a curious fellow, as many writers are, decided to clock their silences. No one spoke for forty-five minutes. Then DiMaggio cleared his throat. Lazzeri turned and said, "Did you say something, Joe?"

"No," broke in Crosetti. "He didn't say nothin'. Now shut up." So we pretty much stayed out of the way of the man the players called the Crow.

At home, Dad's humor depended on whether the Yankees won or what kind of game he had. You kind of walked on eggshells until you knew what his mood was.

Spring training was an entirely different world. There was plenty of free time to go fishing for bass in the

Everglades, and the kids were nearly always included. A bunch of the Yankees went out to the Loxahatchee Canal one morning, and rented a bunch of small motorboats. Mel Stottlemyre and Moose Skowron were among them. Whitey and his boys were in one boat, Dad and his brood in another.

The sun was just coming up. Whitey's boat was about 100 yards from where we were, in an open lake area with all these canals around us. All of a sudden, they started going crazy in the Ford boat. We couldn't figure out what they were doing, so Dad yelled over, "Hey, y'all be quiet. You're going to scare the fish."

We couldn't hear him, but Whitey was waving at us to pull alongside him, so we did. He told us there was a creature in the water, some kind of prehistoric creature, and it kept sticking its head up.

They were freaking out, so we knew it wasn't a joke. Within a minute or so, the creature surfaced again. We learned later that it was a manatee, also known as a sea cow. None of us had ever seen one before, and Dad immediately started digging into his tackle box, where he kept a .38 revolver in case we encountered any alligators.

But he quickly put the weapon away. The manatees are friendly and harmless, plant eaters. This one was fairly typical, dark gray, about fourteen feet long, with a small head with whiskers, a round tail, and two short front legs, paddle-shaped.

As soon as we got over the initial fright, we realized he was not aggressive. He was playful, making walrus sounds, then diving back under. But I have to tell you, it was one hell of a strange sight, especially with the dawn's first light coming up. For a good long moment there we believed that Whitey had indeed discovered a prehistoric monster, and he was none too happy about it.

As the years passed, and Dad was home in the off-season, he started to party more and stay out later. We still had to monitor his moods in the mornings. Billy Martin started to spend an awful lot of time with us in the winters, usually recovering from his marital problems. Mom was less than thrilled, but Dad enjoyed Billy so much she put up with it.

They made up a rule that you had to be a certain age to go anywhere with them, but when I was twelve or thirteen they began taking me on their hunting and fishing trips.

Every winter around Thanksgiving, they hunted on a ranch outside of Kerrville, at a small south Texas town called Leakey. A friend of dad's named Hamilton Wilson owned the ranch, and Harold Youngman had the hunting lease. As the first of the boys to go along, I was designated as their "rookie." They let me have the honor of getting out of the Jeep and opening the gates, so we could be in the blinds before daylight. It was just automatic with Dad and Billy to make up stories intended to scare me. It was uncanny how often they succeeded.

They would tell me about the wild animals that roamed the land and how dangerous they were. It was always watch out for this and watch out for that. Usually we hunted turkey in the morning, in the blinds, and deer in the afternoon. The turkeys were part of the wildlife on the ranch, and you waited in the blind and called them out.

The night before one hunt, we had been talking with Ham Wilson. He told us that there were some javelinas on the land, these large pigs with tusks. They weighed around

400 pounds, and were vicious if they turned and attacked you.

Billy and Dad and Harold decided they wanted to hunt for javelinas in the morning. There was a ravine about a mile off, not much more than a dry creek bed, really, with caves along the sides of it. Ham Wilson told us that the javelinas slept in those caves during the day, but if you went down there you could flush them out.

I had seen the carcasses of javelinas that had been shot down there, so I knew they were around. The road wound its way up and around for about two miles, and the ravine lay below, a mile long. They stopped the Jeep at one end of the ravine, let me out, and handed me a twelve-gauge shotgun with three shells. They told me to walk through the ravine and scare all the javelinas down to the other end, where they would be waiting to pick them off.

Now I was twelve or thirteen, and all I knew was that there were some ugly, hairy, nasty, oversized hogs with tusks who were bound to be in a lousy humor if I yelled and fired off a round and drove them into the open. Well, Billy and Dad and Harold backed up the Jeep and drove to where the ravine and the road crossed, and started circling around to the other end. When they stopped, I was already there, sitting on a rock, holding my shotgun and trying to catch my breath.

I had run all the way and had beat the car getting there. They just cracked up, and I was still huffing too hard to join them. They couldn't believe I had run that fast. I have to admit, I saved a little time by not pausing to make any noise or fire the shotgun.

We never did shoot any javelinas, and after two or three

years I quit going on the hunting trips. I never liked to kill any birds or wild game. The only reason I went in the first place was to spend some extra time with Dad.

In some ways I always thought my father led a charmed life, even when he was abusing it. I was twelve in 1965, when the Yankees met the Houston Astros in an exhibition game that marked the opening of the first covered stadium, the Astrodome.

Mickey Mantle hit the first indoor home run, off Houston's Turk Farrell, in the sixth inning, to break a scoreless tie. Actually, he got the first hit of any kind there leading off the game. Johnny Keane, a Houston resident who had displaced Yogi Berra as manager of the Yankees, had moved Dad to the top of the order to give him the first at bat in the historic new ballpark.

A limousine took the family to the game, and when the driver took ill he left us the keys and went home. The problem was that nobody could remember where the limo was parked, which would not be a big deal on most nights. But this looked like Oscar night in Hollywood. There were at least a hundred limousines lined up at the curb, limos as far as the eye could see. So we just kept walking from one to the next until we found a lock that the keys fit. And, thanking our lucky stars, we drove away to the team's hotel.

We didn't know how lucky. Incredibly, even though the keys fit, we had the wrong limousine. The man who owned or leased the one we drove off finally contacted us, hours later. Our keys fit his, but his keys didn't fit ours.

That type of thing happened to Mickey Mantle all the time.

I was fifteen when my dad's career ended after the 1968 season. The next year, in June, the Yankees flew me to New York to be on the field with him when they retired his number and had a special day for him. Mom and Dad's mother were part of the program, but none of the boys had planned on going. Then the Yankees decided one of us ought to attend, and I flew up alone.

I remember not wanting to go. As a teenager, I figured it would be boring and I'd feel out of place. But I'm glad I went. I couldn't believe how nervous Dad was before the ceremonies started, and how relieved he was when they ended. In between, they kept bringing out one great gift after another—two horses, a motorcycle, a trip to Hawaii. Joe DiMaggio gave him a bronzed plaque with his picture engraved on it that would hang in center field. I don't know how long the fans stood and applauded as a golf cart drove dad around the field, but it must have lasted twenty to twenty-five minutes.

(Another year, at an earlier Mickey Mantle Day at the stadium, I stood near Joe DiMaggio when Robert Kennedy, then a senator from New York, popped into the dugout to shake hands with the players. DiMaggio maneuvered himself behind another player, and Kennedy walked past him.

(Even then, as a kid, I knew there was tension in the air, but hadn't a clue as to what it was. Years later, I read that Joe believed there had been a romance between his ex-wife, Marilyn Monroe, and Bobby Kennedy.)

The winter after the Yankees retired his Number 7, he had been in Florida for an appearance and then flew into Love Field, at the time the only airport Dallas had. Luckily,

Tony Lema and Jackie Cupit, two of the best pro golfers of that era, were on the same flight and saw how much he had to drink. They offered to drive him home, and when he refused they followed him in their car. His luck held. He didn't make it home, but skidded on a road slick with sleet, went over a curb, and blew out a tire. When they dropped him off, Tony and Jackie made him promise not to leave the house and try to go back and get his car.

Right after they left, so did he. We rode double on the motorcycle the Yankees had given him. I fixed the flat, then he said, "Okay, now you get in front so I can keep an eye on you going home." I was only sixteen, but there was no way I was going to let him get behind me. It was too cold to keep arguing, so he finally agreed to go first. I followed him home on the motorcycle and we made it safely.

After Dad quit playing baseball, we teamed up to play a lot of golf. I had some talent for the game and could hit the ball about 250 yards when I was ten. He sent me to one of the best teachers in the country, Florene Hager of Dallas, for lessons. Her daughter, Nancy, was one of the country's finest amateur players. Her son, Joey, was on the PGA tour a few years later.

The first year I worked with her she took the woods out of my bag and wouldn't let me use them. That really ticked me off because, like my Dad, I always wanted to hit the long ball. But Florene taught me the swing, inside and out. To this day, if I hit a ball wrong I can feel in my swing what I did to cause it.

Dad and I were a pretty good pair, and we played some fairly high-stakes golf games against the members at Preston Trail, and on our trips to Oklahoma and Missouri.

We'd play scrambles, where you both hit two shots and play the best one.

Once, Dad and Billy Martin and I played three of the best golfers in Joplin. We were down about $500 going into Number 14, and Dad turned to me in the cart and said, "What the hell is wrong with you?" I said, "Well, hell, we're getting beat, I'm playing lousy, and it's a lot of money."

He said, "Hey, I can sign a dozen baseballs and get that money back. Loosen up and just play your game."

Billy made a putt on the last hole and we ended up winning the match. We had half the club's membership following us around as a gallery. It was a pretty nice moment. It also showed that Dad had some sharp insights into the competitive mind. He knew I was pressing, thinking about the money, and he tried to put me at ease.

The most fun was during a fantasy camp in 1989, when we played the Fords, Whitey and his sons, Tommy and Eddie, against the Mantles. Either Danny or David joined Dad and me. We were beating them one day, but they had won a hole and were starting to come back on us. We were on the green, pretty close to the hole. Whitey had a lake between him and the green, and Eddie was standing next to a sprinkler head, close to the yard marker.

Whitey said, "How far are we to the hole?"

Instead of moving to get a closer look, Eddie bent over and cocked his head sideways. Then he called out, "Looks like sixty-six yards."

Whitey took out a club, dropped his shot about twenty yards short, and then walked over to the marker. He cut loose a stream of expletives at Eddie and said, "Look at that sign again. It says ninety-nine, not sixty-six."

It was around this time that I wound up being sent off to military school. I didn't care much for school. I had been skipping classes, just sliding by. I think Mom and Dad wanted to get me away from the group of people I was running with, and get me headed in a better direction. They picked an excellent school, Riverside Military Academy, which had a split campus, with classes half the year in Gainesville, Georgia, and the other half in Hollywood, Florida.

I spent my sophomore year there and, looking back, wish I had stayed. I probably would have done much better, gone on to college, and played baseball. But I didn't. This was in 1969 and 1970, at the height of the Vietnam War, and military schools were not much in favor. I went back to Dallas and got a General Equivalency Diploma.

The one special result that came out of my year at Riverside was that I went out for baseball and made the all-state team as a center fielder. It was the only season of organized ball, at any level, that I had played up to that point. My dad was in his last year with the Yankees, and their camp in Fort Lauderdale was thirty miles away from our spring campus in Hollywood.

If he knew we were playing, he would drive the thirty miles from the Yankee camp in Fort Lauderdale. On long weekends, he would come by and "break me out" for a little rest and recreation.

We played our games in the late afternoons, after the class schedule. My heart would jump when I'd see his white Lincoln pull into the parking lot. He always watched from the car. Anyone else's father could get out of the car and sit in the stands, but for him it wasn't possible.

I didn't feel what I would describe as pressure when he showed up. His being there picked up my play and made me want to excel.

We played on a diamond that had no fences, and there were trees along the back of the field about 400 feet from home plate. I made what was probably one of the best catches of my life on a day when he was watching from his car. It was the last play of the game, and I made a running, over-the-shoulder, one-handed catch all the way to the tree line. It was one of the sweetest feelings I ever felt in my life.

After the game, Dad smiled and said, "Good catch." He was paying me two compliments. One, he acknowledged the catch and, two, he paid me the respect of not reacting with astonishment. His words told me that was the kind of catch I was capable of making, and he wasn't surprised.

Ideally, if I could rewrite the script, I would have stuck with baseball. I had so little experience to draw on, but I had one quality my Dad never had: patience. If he didn't catch on to something real quick, he would get frustrated and walk away. I have the same short temper he had, but I work on mine.

Baseball came so easily to him, patience didn't need to be a part of his makeup. He was a natural. He was helpless when it came to figuring out how any kind of machinery worked. The first time he bought a cellular phone, he almost threw it away. He had to keep asking people how to turn it on. His frustration with anything he couldn't pick up quickly was almost comic.

Dad never pushed any of us toward baseball and, in fact, encouraged my love of golf. He didn't want to see us suffer the endless comparisons, or face the prospect of rejection. He knew that we hadn't been prepared or groomed for the game, the way his father had groomed him.

But without ever saying so, I believe he really wanted one of us to give baseball a try, and I turned out to be the one. I had only one high school season behind me, and no real training in the fundamentals. There was really nothing else happening in my life.

As if I didn't have enough handicaps to begin with, I was already twenty-four. In baseball, that makes you a late, late starter.

This is what I had going for me: I grew up around the New York Yankees when they were baseball's last great team. I had speed, good hands, good instincts. Most of all, I was Mickey Mantle's son and I had at least a slice of his raw talent. I wanted to find out if that was enough.

If you were looking for an example of the extremes in baseball, the glory and the grind, the penthouse and the outhouse, you would have it in the careers of the two Mickey Mantles. His career lasted eighteen years and took him to the Hall of Fame. Mine lasted less than two years and took me to three cities, none higher than Class A. But I know why I failed, and I don't feel any shame about it. In fact, I'm glad I made the attempt, and it made me appreciate my dad, and his teammates, all the more. In a low-rent way, I came to identify with them.

It was 1977 when I decided I wanted to take a crack at pro baseball. Dad kept testing me, asking if I was sure this what I wanted, if I knew what kind of challenge I was setting for myself. He really wanted me to think about it before we left for Florida.

Billy Martin was managing the Yankees and Dad was going to camp as a batting instructor. He took me with him, three weeks before the minor league camp was to start. Neither of them wanted anyone to know who I was, so no one would give me a hard time. They knew it might come off as a lark or a gimmick or even what it was, a long-shot experiment. No one wanted this to turn into a kind of publicity stunt, least of all me, so the equipment man issued me a jersey without a number.

I worked out with the major leaguers every day, shagging flies in the outfield, taking batting practice in the cage. Based on what I heard, I looked pretty good. I got about a three-week jump on everybody at the minor league camp, and no one blew my identity. A lot of people started asking about me, Who was the kid without a number? Billy would say, "Aw, he's nobody," or he would change the subject.

I was assigned to the Yankees' farm club at Fort Lauderdale, meaning that I just moved over to the minor league complex. Now I had a uniform number, 76, and my name was no longer a secret.

I stayed with the Class A team for most of the spring, about two months, and never got into a game. Not as a starter, not as a sub, not as a pinch hitter or baserunner. Not for an inning. Not for a pitch. I kept my mouth shut, but whatever edge I gained in the major league camp had ebbed away.

The manager never said a word to me, but it wasn't hard to figure out what he was doing. He felt the Yankees had pushed Mickey Mantle's kid on him, a really green pea, with a year of high school ball behind him. He had to carry me on the roster, but he didn't have to play me.

Then Billy Martin came to one of our games, after the Yankees had finished working out, and spotted me on the bench. He took me aside and asked, "How come you're not playing today?"

I said, "I never play. Any day. The guy doesn't use me. All I've done since I got here is sit on the bench."

I could see Billy's eyes getting flinty. He said, "All right, Two Dogs, go on back over there and sit down. I'll look into this."

That was his nickname for me, Two Dogs. It was part of the punch line of a joke that Billy and my dad enjoyed telling. A little Indian boy was curious because his mother was getting ready to give birth. He looked out a window and asked, "Father, why do we Indians have such unusual names? Like Two Fawns Running, Two Eagles Soaring, Two Lions Fighting?"

His dad said, "Well, the names are chosen from the first thing the father sees after the mother gives birth. That's how we name the child. Why do you ask, Two Dogs F-----g?"

I saw Billy and my manager talking and it was clear to me that he wasn't sharing any of his favorite jokes. Billy was pissed. But it was clear to him now that the Yankees' farm system wasn't the best place for me to break in. The Fort Lauderdale club had better and younger prospects than me—Pat Tabler and Willie McGee, to name a couple. I needed to learn the game. That meant making mistakes, and my name was going to be held against me.

A week later, I was traded to Plant City, the Texas Rangers' Class A team in the Florida State League. I got into a few games, made some plays, hit the ball hard now and then, but would have led the league in strikeouts if they had played me every day. They traded me to an independent team in Alexandria, Virginia, and I got to open the season with them the next year.

My manager was Les Peden, a former big league catcher with the Senators who had played against my dad. He liked me, wanted me to do well, and saw what I was up against. The first day I showed up for camp, you couldn't get through the press to reach the clubhouse. It was sick, considering how little I had done.

But there were things I really enjoyed about life in the low minors, and not the ones you might expect. My chances might have been better if I really needed to live on what they were paying us, and if I had to make it or go back to the lead mines, the options that my dad faced.

I wasn't Michael Jordan. I hadn't proved a damned thing in any sport and I couldn't rent luxury buses for the team to travel on. I wanted to be part of the team and I lived on the same scale everyone else did. We were paid $500 a month and in Alexandria, which is right across the Potomac River from Washington, D.C., that didn't go very far. So five of us had to chip in to rent a one-bedroom apartment and five rollaway beds. This was in the Carolina League, and we had bus rides of up to ten hours from one town to the next.

Once, in Lynchburg, we got into town on a Thursday and were rained out the entire weekend. There were a couple of girls' colleges in town and finally, by Saturday night, we had hooked up with some coeds. The party got out of hand, apparently, because the Holiday Inn kicked us out and we had to spend the night on the team bus.

Mickey Jr.

I was struggling at bat and playing poorly on the road, but I had my moments. One night in Alexandria the fog rolled in and they called the game after seven innings. Just before they called it, you could barely see the guy standing in the batter's box. Once the ball left his bat, you couldn't see it.

I was playing left field, and heard the *thonk* of the bat against the ball. It was lost in the fog, but I ran to where I thought it would be and the ball dropped right in my glove. My instincts were not the problem. Mike Ferrara, who was a scout for the Yankees, told me I got as good a jump off the bat as anybody he had ever seen.

But I had a weakness I couldn't conceal. I could crush a fastball, but I couldn't hit a curve, which came from having played so little. Pitchers aren't dumb. Even in the bush leagues, once they knew I had trouble hitting a curve, that was all I ever saw.

On the road one night, I struck out four straight times. An old drunk in the stands had been riding me all night. As I walked back to the dugout, he yelled, "Why don't you go home and tell your daddy how you're playing?" The next thing I knew I was in the stands and going after the guy. There was a big brawl and it took about five of my teammates to break it up.

We got everything settled down and that night, at the hotel, the manager stopped my hotel room. He said, "You're not having much fun doing this, are you?"

I said, "No, I'm really not."

He said, "Well, you need to take a break. I'm not going to play you anymore on this road trip. I'd like you to think about whether this is really what you want to do. Let me know when you get back to Alexandria."

I knew my dad had been keeping tabs on me, watching the box scores. I called him that night and told him I thought I was just taking up somebody else's space. I don't think I said anything that surprised him. He knew it was going to be hard. You don't find very many twenty-four-year-olds walking out of an insurance office and making it big in baseball. In the low minors, most of them are rookies, just out of high school, and they are obsessed with two things: making it to the majors and tits.

Dad didn't second-guess or lecture me. He just told me to get my golf clubs back out and start playing golf.

I was hitting .193 when I left Alexandria. And yet I wouldn't have traded any of it, the people I met, the times we had. Even with a mediocre team, and a lot of guys who were going nowhere, we bonded and believed in each other. I could see how players with a winning team, a World Series team, would become so close. Like my dad said of his teammates, who won all those pennants for the Yankees, they were his brothers.

Just on the teams I played on, the two years I played, you go through a lot on and off the field. You are thrown together by circumstances and chance. It becomes a surrogate family. I never saw any of the guys argue. We all got along.

And I believe most of my teammates, and many of the fans, were rooting for me. If I had started earlier, had come up a harder way, the outcome might have been different. But in the end, I didn't mind recognizing that there was only one Mickey Mantle.

I'm actually a little taller than dad was, but not as broad and not nearly as strong. His forearms were huge, and few athletes are blessed with his eye–hand coordination. He always said his strength came from milking cows and working in the mines. He broke up the rocks with a sledge-hammer as they came down the conveyor belt.

I never imagined myself trying to compete with my father, except possibly on the golf course. Once we had a home run contest at the fantasy camp, with some of the campers, Dad, and myself. I won it with three homers to his two. I was kidding him later at dinner and he didn't want to talk about it. He really didn't. I kind of let that drop. He hated to lose. If he was pitching pennies at a crack, he expected to win.

He was careful about what he said in public, but he felt strongly that the trends in baseball have all but ruined the game he loved. When he broke in with the Yankees, the players were together for most of their career. They looked forward to seeing each other at spring training in Florida. It was like a reunion.

Dad faulted himself for not staying in shape early in his career, but the truth is few of those players did. Off-season programs didn't exist. In Dad's day, they even worried about getting muscle-bound. Today you see and hear about guys maintaining a weight program all winter long. You read about Don Mattingly having a batting cage in his house. Cal Ripken Jr. built his own gymnasium. You read about Nolan Ryan doing forty-five minutes on a stationary bike after he pitched a no-hitter.

What dad really kicked himself about was not rehabbing his injuries. But the knee operations in his time were primitive compared to today's techniques. They cut into your tendons, and left a scar that looked like a zipper.

Today they can deal with many of the problems with a 'scope—an arthroscopic procedure that for a jock is the biggest advance since doctors quit using leeches.

But, yeah, Dad would have prolonged his career if he had pushed himself harder after his surgeries. But when he was young, it was easy to feel invincible and believe that talent would see you through.

He never said so in public, but he didn't forgive the players for the strike that canceled the playoffs and World Series in 1994, and spring training in 1995. He thought the money they made was sheer lunacy, but he hesitated to say it in public because he always felt guilty about getting money for signing his name. But he didn't mind if a guy made five or ten million a year, if he earned it. He thought they ought to start paying the players year-to-year, with a standard base and bonuses for performance. We'd watch baseball games on TV, and it drove him crazy to see guys making millions who looked for reasons not to play.

No one ever said that about Mickey Mantle. The team doctors would examine one of his injuries and suggest that he ought to be in a hospital. Casey Stengel would talk about how Dad would go to him and say, "I want to play."

He missed the games, the guys, the clubhouse, and he never found anything to replace them. I was about nineteen or twenty when I started traveling with him. I worked on his schedule, filled orders for some of his collectibles, confirmed his arrangements, returned some of his calls. That was when we started drinking together. In Florida, when Billy Martin helped out with the fantasy camps, they would keep me out until about two o'clock in the morning, knowing that I was the one who had to be on the field by nine-thirty. They got a kick out of watching me throw up after running wind sprints in the outfield.

I don't know if we drank out of boredom or habit, but as senseless as it was, we had some rowdy good times at the baseball camps. One night, after we finished a game, Dad and I drove down the Intracoastal Waterway to a place called Stan's. We took some beer out of the team freezer at the ballpark and drank all day. Then we went back to the hotel and picked up Moose Skowron, Hank Bauer, and John Blanchard. We were all pretty soused.

The next morning, Dad was on the phone wanting to know where the hell the rental car was. I honestly didn't know. But Moose had driven me back to the hotel and I told Dad if anyone knew, he should. Moose thought he had parked the car in the lot, but he wasn't certain.

There was always a cop at the entrance to the ballpark, so we figured we'd have some fun with Skowron. We got the cop to walk into the coaches' dressing room and ask if Moose Skowron was there. Then he handcuffed him and said he was under arrest for losing the rental car.

We had a quick laugh and the cop went on his way. The weird part is, we never did find the car. Never saw it again. To this day we don't know if it was stolen, or if it's still sitting in the wrong parking lot somewhere in Florida.

We all felt badly about it, and our remorse wasn't helped any by the fact that we all had hangovers. I was sitting on the bench when someone said one team was short-handed and I had to play in that day's game. I went to bat and hit a long home run and Dad sent someone to bring the ball back. He said something like, "That's pretty tough to do when you're feeling like snail shit."

Not long ago, I was going through some personal effects and I ran across that baseball. Dad had written on it, "Nice home run. Now you're only 535 behind me." I've had that ball close to ten years, I guess, and it means as much as anything he ever gave me.

I never intended to make Dad my career. But for a long time I had no idea what I wanted to do. I went to junior college in Dallas, sold life insurance, worked for an oil company, took classes and got a real estate license. So did he. We never did anything with it. If anything, he made things too easy for my brothers and me. He was always handing out money. When we won a bet on the golf course, he let me have it. If we lost, he paid the debt. He never made it hard for me, never as hard as he probably should have.

From the reaction I read and heard, many were touched by it when Dad said, "If my father had been his father, Mickey Jr. would have been a big leaguer." I'm not so sure. More likely, if Dad had cooped me up in the back yard for three or four hours every day, playing catch and pitching to me, I would have run away from home.

Really, when he was a kid there wasn't much else to do, not in Commerce. Television wasn't what it is today. Shopping malls didn't exist, not in Oklahoma, and neither did freeways. How do you compare eras, much less parents?

I'm not sure he realized how unusual it was that his father invested all of his hopes in Mick, maybe at the expense of his other children. And when Grandpa died, this twenty-year-old country boy, with one magnificent gift, took over the entire family. He was their summer wishes and winter dreams. What if he didn't make it? How were they going to manage? That was a fairly tall responsibility, I'd say.

But he never thought of his life in terms of the obligations he met and kept. He used to tell me that he blamed himself for my drinking problem, for not finishing college, for having an unstable marriage that ended in divorce. I tried to get through to him, Hey, let me keep a little of my own guilt.

The odds were probably against Cindy and me from the moment we decided to get married. I don't know what we really expected. She was pretty, and had qualities I didn't have that I thought would help me. She was motivated, driven in a way I wasn't. I don't think Cindy realized what she was getting into when she married the Mantle family. You got the whole package, all of us, and the wheelers and dealers attracted by Dad's name.

The night we told my parents we were flying to Las Vegas to get married, neither one of them said anything. Mom looked like she wanted to faint. Whatever the reason, didn't believe the marriage would work. It didn't. Our divorce, in 1992, left scars. But it also left us a treasure, our daughter, Mallory.

Mom held our family together. That was never a secret. But Dad was right about a lot of things, too. I look at David and Danny and where I am today, and I see that some of the kids we ran around with are dead from doing drugs. He kept after us, and never let up, about kicking drugs. I told him dope to our generation was like alcohol to his. He always made the same argument: "Yeah, but it isn't against the law to drink." And he was right. He didn't like the sleazy grade of characters associated with it, either.

For what seemed to me a long time, four or five years, I

was the one who did the traveling and the hanging out with him. After I got married, Danny filled my place. Of the four of us, Danny and I understood each other. Billy had a chip on his shoulder, although none of us doubted that he had good reasons for it. David was the sensitive one, a little more of a beatnik. Each in his turn gave Dad his support. If he was in really bad shape, we'd be there to pick him up, literally. We'd help him off a plane, or out of a bar, or get him home. When he and Billy Martin were in their marathon drinking days, it was touchy work.

Unlike Billy, when Dad drank he didn't get physical, he didn't turn into Jack Dempsey, although he threatened to—especially if you were trying to help him. All the boys had a confrontation or two with Dad, but there wasn't one swing taken, not one. One night he seemed more determined than usual to bait me into a fight, but I told him, "You can kick the hell out of me if you want, and you'll feel bad about it tomorrow. But I'll never hit you back." We never fought. Most of the time I would just shut up and walk away. We were so much alike.

When I think of all the close brushes each of us had with real disaster, I tend to go back and count our blessings. I was in a bar with David and his friends the night he had the accident that almost killed him. They were going to see a concert and wanted me to join them. I said, No, I'm not getting in a car.

They had just left the bar when a guy topped a hill going sixty and crashed into them head-on. If they hadn't been in a big car, a Caddy, David probably would have been killed. As it was, they had to fuse his spine and he was unconscious off and on for three days.

Those were the worst of times for Dad. He felt so help-less if one of his sons was sick or hurt. He had a phobia about hospitals and he worried about not knowing what to do or say. He beat himself up over things he couldn't con-trol. When he was proud of us, he gave Mom the credit. When he won an award for the career he had, or the records he set, he gave his dad the credit, or his teammates, or the skills God gave him. When anything went wrong, he took the blame the way he reached for a check.

Out of all the things he did, the World Series teams he starred on, the home runs he hit, the records he broke, his induction into the Hall of Fame, what I admired him for the most was getting sober.

He had gone through those years like one of those World War I fighter planes in a nosedive. He couldn't pull out of it, and after a while he didn't try. He talked about the leisure time they had to kill, flying on planes, sitting around hotels. Waiting was always one of the hardest things for him to do. Drinking filled up those hours. And well-intended people made it easy for him. His fans sent drinks to his table, round after round. The hotel manage-ment sent complimentary bottles of wine or Scotch or vodka to his room.

I don't think he ever would have gone to the Betty Ford Center if Danny hadn't done it first. I know how hard it was for him to make that decision. I was the last member of the family to get sober, and I'm not proud of that status. But what counts is that we did.

After his return from Betty Ford, the real change I saw in him was how he dealt with the public. He became more tolerant. Before, when we were out drinking, he would embarrass you by telling someone to take a hike, in language that was raw. After he was in treatment, I never saw him treat anyone rudely, or swear in front of them..

We still played golf together, and it didn't trouble him if other people were drinking around him. We would pass a drink cart and he would ask me if I wanted a beer. He didn't put any pressure on me to quit, but once in a while he would say, "I wish you would."

He had never talked to me about his going to the Betty Ford Center. I heard him ask Danny a few times about what it was like, not drinking. I could see that Dad was getting worse. It didn't take nearly as much booze anymore to put him in no-man's-land.

From the time he came back from Palm Springs in February 1994, he kept saying he never came close to taking another drink and was tempted only once. I didn't believe him. Now that I've been through it, I know he was being truthful. I thought I would have a craving, but it wasn't there. I didn't miss it because I had grown tired of waking up every morning feeling so rotten. I was tired of being sick and tired.

Dad looked better than he had in years, and he said he felt better. We were all optimistic about the happy years he had ahead of him. But he had passed the point of no return. He wasn't going to be able to turn back the clock. He had played for years on crippled knees, but he couldn't outrun the injury he had done to his system.

I believe he was in pain for most of his last year. In April 1994, we drove to Austin to play in Darrell Royal's golf tournament. We got there a day early and played with Coach Royal and a couple of his friends. He didn't feel well on the golf course, and he admitted to me later that he was having stomach cramps. It was nothing serious, he said.

He had been bothered by an ulcer for years and was often popping Tagamets or Rolaids, so a stomachache didn't raise any red flags. The tournament lasted two days, and he only came out of his room to sit by one of the holes and hit a tee shot. That was the tourney where he would bet any players who came along that he could get closer on a par three. If they won, he gave them an autographed baseball. If he won, they paid $150 for it. By the end of the day, he had raised $13,000 for charity.

Even before he checked into Betty Ford, Marshall Smith, who ran Dad's golf tournament in Oklahoma, took him to a clinic in Tulsa. They ran him through a battery of tests, including the barium enema, all of your basic nightmares. Nothing showed up.

I could tell when he was hurting. Something was wrong, and this time he knew it was more than an ulcer. He told me, "You know, Mick, what I'm doing now, this isn't really living."

He would get bloated from retaining fluid. The liver wasn't working properly. He wouldn't let us know, but the doctors had warned him. The damage could not be reversed.

He put up a front for us, but the year he was sober wasn't really a good one. It was sad because everybody had the same hope for him: That he would come through his recovery and have another ten to fifteen years with a good quality of life.

The three of us—Danny, David, and me—took turns

staying with him in the hospital, sleeping on the couch that folded into a bed in his suite. We never left him alone. I happened to be the one who was with him the night they found out a new liver had come in and they took him to the operating room.

I didn't know if I would ever see him again, if he would make it through the surgery. At that point they were guessing he had perhaps two days to live. He was as yellow as a manila envelope. From the foot of the bed you couldn't see his shoulders because his stomach was swollen and bloated. That night, when they rolled him out, I said, "We'll see you later."

He said, "Okay, see you later, partner." Those might have been the last words he said to me. I thought of a hundred other things we might have said. It was, of course, what one writer called an "unconscious reenactment" of man's inability to say good-bye.

I went back to sleep. They kept him in the Intensive Care Unit for three days on a respirator. The doctors said the operation was a success and everybody's hopes soared, especially when they kept looking for signs of the liver being rejected and that never happened. They did say they were afraid they might not have gotten all the cancer, that some of the cells had gotten into the bile ducts, and they might spread. Which is exactly what happened.

There was very little time to share any deep or final thoughts after the surgery. First we were sure he was going to be well and the personal sentiments could wait. Then, when the pains came back and he returned to the hospital for the last time, he was sedated much of the time.

But in between his hospital stays, he tried to talk to me

from his heart. We were in the clubhouse at Preston Trails. He was able to ride the stationary bike, walking a little, looking forward to getting into shape. He had never talked to me as intently as he did that day. He had never asked so much of me.

He asked me to promise him I would go to the Betty Ford Center. He told me what it would mean to him, and to me. I was silent while he talked and I turned my gaze to the window. I realized later that this was the exact pose that Roy True described, when he half-laughed, half-complained about Dad's attention span when there were business matters to discuss, or hard news to explain.

When Roy stopped talking, Dad would turn to face him and say, "Is that it?" Roy would nod and say, "That's it." Dad would get up and head for the door, and give his assent with a curt, "Okay."

Now I was striking exactly the same pose, and I hadn't actually answered him. I heard Dad ask, "Did you hear me?"

I said, "Yeah, I heard you."

"Well, what do you think?"

I shrugged my shoulders. I knew if I kept going the way I was going, I would be throwing my life away. But I couldn't bring up the words. I couldn't make him a promise I wasn't yet certain I could keep. I didn't want to tell him I would, and then not do it. I had been drinking, and doing the drugs, since I was fifteen or sixteen years old. I didn't know if I could function without it. If I got sober, how would I respond when I was around alcohol? I didn't want to be the one who let everybody else down, including myself. So I said nothing.

He leaned closer to me and looked into my eyes. "You're a coldhearted sonofabitch," he said.

I wasn't offended. There was affection and respect mixed in with his appraisal. He knew he was seeing himself. He also knew that it was going to happen, but in my own time. That was why he didn't keep pushing, didn't back me into a corner. I always reacted the way he did to being pushed: I turned the other way.

I had told him earlier that I would go when I knew I was ready. When I went, I wanted to make it work. I had already cut way back. I had cut out the drugs completely, had slowed down the drinking. Everyone else in the family had stopped and, frankly, I had lost a lot of camaraderie. I didn't want to rejoin society and slip, and be the one who failed. He understood that in my way, I had given him my word.

We were not really sparring. And I don't want this to sound like the Psychic Hotline, but we could reach each other's thoughts. He had been brought up a certain way, and if he couldn't deal with his feelings he buried them. He paid a high cost for packing away the affection that was so close to his surface.

For most of our lives, when we greeted each other after a separation of weeks or months, we would shake hands. It wasn't just him. Everybody in his family, my uncles, his cousins, kept the same distance.

I know the conversation I described doesn't make me sound like Mr. Warmth. But Dad freed me to enjoy the kind of closeness that had come so hard to us. Five or six times a day, my daughter Mallory and I hug and say we love each other.

He knew I would make that trip and I can't lash myself for not saying the words. Sometimes you speak with a look or a gesture. Nothing made a stronger impression on me than when he threw back the cover and sheets on his hospital bed and said, "Please, Mick, don't let this happen to you. Take better care of yourself. I don't want to you wind up like I did."

I was so used to seeing him, thinking of him, as sinewy and strong. Now he had lost so much weight, the flesh was hanging from his arms. His legs were so swollen the skin was cracking. It was hard for me to see Mickey Mantle like that. And I know it was hard for him to have old friends see him that way.

But I will never forget how his former teammates reacted to him when they filed into his room. Whitey, Moose, Hank, John Blanchard, Tony Kubek. Bobby Richardson, who went into the ministry after he left baseball, came back the next day and prayed with him. I could see it in Dad's face; he was comfortable with what was going to happen. I give Bobby a lot of credit for that.

The former Yankees were visibly shaken by the way he looked. But they treated him with such respect, such tenderness, that for a few minutes the pain and the years were just stripped away.

Death came to him just after midnight, an hour he knew so well, on Sunday, August 13, 1995. I made up my mind to enter the Betty Ford Center in October. I planned it as carefully as I could; I played in a golf tournament the first three days of the month, took my last drink, and had a week to detox.

I hadn't known until later how much suspense surrounded Dad's decision. There were a lot of people going through that pins-and-needles stage, wondering if he would get on the plane or not. They knew if he did he would go through recovery. He never quit on anything in his life.

My flight was to leave at three o'clock on a Sunday afternoon, and as I was getting ready to board the plane, just across from the gate there was a bar with a television and the Dallas Cowboys football game was coming on. I thought, "Damn, I could just sit down at that bar, have a couple beers and miss the flight." Well, I didn't. I don't know why I didn't. But I got on the plane and flew to California. I'll be eternally glad that I did.

Christmas 1995 was the first that I can actually say I had a good holiday with Mallory. I actually sat there and put toys together with her and enjoyed the day. Any other time, I had a hangover or had just gotten in from a night of drinking. I wasn't there for her emotionally. I knew what it was like to have to worry about being quiet because Daddy didn't feel well.

She loved Dad, of course, and called him Papa Mickey. She drew a handmade get-well card and gave it to him in the hospital. When you saw him with his two granddaughters, or doing one of his impulsive acts of kindness, you knew he had a heart as big as a Number 5 washtub.

In the program at Betty Ford, there is a lot of emphasis put on opening up and sharing. I had a hard time with that; I wasn't used to letting my anger or frustrations out. I just held them inside. They told me that was why I probably drank as much as I did.

I had two roommates while I was there. The second

one had been there before, when my dad was in recovery. He said that my dad had mentioned one day that he wished Mickey Jr. would come out there.

I can imagine myself having a conversation with him, telling him, "Well, Dad, I did go and I made it."

And he would grin and say, "Good catch."

Chapter 7

David

David is our spiritual son, the one most likely to go off to India or Tibet in search of a wise man. He can be the funniest and the most tiring member of the family. He is hyper and reflective. He thinks up poems while he rides a Harley-Davidson. After Mick's death, he grew a goatee and thought about getting a tattoo. He said he was trying to find his identity and he thought his father would approve. I don't think so, but before it could become a family issue he shaved off the goatee and put the tattoo on hold.

—*MERLYN*

November 10, 1995

Dad,

I'm writing this letter to let you know some of my feelings, and try to understand what went on the last three months of your life.

One thing you taught me is no matter what, never give up. There is always hope. I'm so glad I was by your side at the hospital. I can remember coming to see you in the Intensive Care Unit after the operation. I told you I loved you and you told me you loved me, too. I have been asked if you ever told me that and now I can say, yes. It meant a lot to me.

At times I think I'm in denial about your death; that you are on another road trip, I guess because that was almost your whole life, living out of a suitcase.

I really haven't had time to grieve for you, we've been so busy. At first, I was angry, bitter and downright mad. I had thoughts of giving up and to start using again. I'm glad I didn't. I felt a part of me died, also. Is that self-pity or selfishness? Or maybe it's just that I miss you.

I told the press in an early interview that I do mourn you as a father, not as an idol, American hero or whatever. Nobody has given me a chance to grieve. During a press conference I lost it, and cried. Afterwards, a female reporter asked why. My answer was, it took a year to feel comfortable with Billy's death and here you had been gone five weeks.

A very important fact is my being with you that last night you were alive, holding your hand and telling you I loved you and everything will be fine. This was a blessing for me. I thought if I wasn't there I would really beat myself up for feeling guilty.

I've had questions, too, if I did everything possible that night to save you. The doctor said there was nothing I could have done. I just felt it was my turn to take care of you. I know if I wasn't clean and sober I could not be in control of myself. I know I need to find time to cry and accept that you will not be coming back.

One thing I am very proud of is knowing I will be able to help the Recovery Program and the Organ Donor Program because of our family name. Reflecting on our father-son relationship, it wasn't perfect. At times, I wished we did not have to share you with the rest of the world, even at the funeral service. I wonder, where does the price of fame stop? Or the obligations to the public?

Thank God the funeral wasn't a circus, like all the years we were in our disease. Miracles do happen.

Your little Miss America is getting ready to have her second birthday Sunday. You'd be proud of her. If she sees a picture of you, she says "Papa." I'm glad you got to know her a little.

I had a dream about you the other night, the first one. I think it is because I miss you, and started to realize you won't be coming back. I agree with mom—you died with dignity and honor. I'm kind of at a stopping point, in this letter, not my life. I have your memory to help with that.

I will always love and think of you,

Your son, David

P.S.—Everybody thought I was going to totally lose it, but I did not, to my surprise, also. I know it's not wrong to feel sorrow and pain. I'm a stronger person than we all thought.

When you go into recovery, you are encouraged to write letters: to yourself, your father, mother, friends, enemies, fictional characters. It doesn't matter. The important thing is that you often find it easier to put on paper thoughts you could never say out loud.

I have a sheet of yellow, lined notebook paper that my dad was going to use for one of his letters. He came up with a great title, or introduction, but that was as far as he got. The words at the top of the page say,

"A Letter to the Drunk Who Shares My Body."

His wife and his sons know what he meant. We all had to do some double-bunking while we tried to get rid of our addictions. There is a special joy in facing your problems and letting the process of healing begin. If you have never been a drunk, I'm not sure you can appreciate the feeling. It's like Dean Martin is supposed to have said: "The trouble with being sober is, when you wake up in the morning you know that's as good as you're going to feel all day."

When I was at the Betty Ford Center, in the fall of 1993, I was asked in a group session how I felt. You are always being asked to express your feelings. I said, "Magical," and people laughed at the exuberance of it. All I meant was, I felt I could do anything that day. I was getting free of the drugs and alcohol, something that struck me as positive and exhilarating. That was a very nice day for me.

None of us wanted to bring any dishonor to the Mantle name, which is one reason none of us went into baseball, although Mickey Jr. had the talent. Even Dad thought so. One way or another, we mucked it up some by not leading clean or useful lives. We've tried hard the past few years, just as Dad did, to make up for those mistakes. I know Dad will be remembered as the great baseball player who inspired so many people, including some who were not even Yankee fans.

I'm not sure when I first heard the term "a dysfunctional family." I'm not sure when I realized that was us. I hope the final judgment will show that we overcame our difficulties, especially the ones that were self-inflicted. We have always been bonded; now we're closer than ever and trying to carry on the good works Dad had pledged to do before he died.

Except for Billy, whose problems turned out to be terminal, I was the son Dad worried about the most. After we all got sober, he would still ask Danny, "Is David okay? Is he doing anything?" And Danny would say, "No, Dad, he's fine. He's just full of nervous energy."

When you go into treatment, they tell you each child has a different role. I was the clown, the one who wants to make everybody laugh. I'm also the one who writes poetry and thinks dark thoughts. For most of his life, Mickey Mantle landed on his feet. I was the one who kept landing on his head.

I've had migraine headaches ever since I was in a bad motorcycle accident a few years ago. In November 1995, I was diagnosed as having attention deficit disorder (ADD) and obsessive-compulsive behavior. That should not have surprised anyone. As children, Billy and I were both dyslexic, and those disorders often go together.

I might have been a much better student if the professionals had figured this out thirtysomething years ago. What surprised me was when the nurse asked, "How many times have you been hit in the head?" I doubt that question is on the standard form when you take a physical. I don't know if she picked it up from looking at me or from reading the X rays. But the answer is at least seven. I've had surgery to fuse the bone in my neck where it joins the spine.

There were a couple of motorcycle accidents, two fights—in one I was hit with a helmet, the other with a baseball bat—and at least two car wrecks. The doctors changed my medication and I'm doing fine now. There really isn't a great deal wrong with me that can't be cured by coming to terms with my father's death. I just never realized it would be so hard or take so long.

Another question the nurse asked was, Did I have any sixth sense awareness? At times, I feel that I do. She asked if I pick up the scent or fragrance of an absent person. On the way home, in the cab of my truck, I could smell the aftershave lotion Dad last used. It was called "Fahrenheit."

I guess I ought to get this out of the way right now. When he died, I went through a period of not wanting to live, either. I always wondered how I would face it when he was gone, and when it happened something inside me died, too. I was really confused, my mind going in circles. One minute I thought he was going to be alive and well and a new man, and two months later he was dead.

He had a unique chance to make everything right, and fate sort of jumped in. I spent a lot of nights at the hospital with him, and so did Danny. I started blaming myself. I thought maybe I had done something wrong the last few days; maybe I gave him too much medication. Crazy thoughts.

As he was dying, I felt that my own life was worthless. My mind felt scattered, which probably was related to the ADD. There were pressures. I spent so much time at the hospital, I neglected my wife and little girl.

But I must not have thought too hard about suicide, because I never attempted anything. The closest I came was when I played Russian roulette, one night while Dad was dying. It didn't occur to me how close to death I was. I pulled the trigger twice and the chamber was empty. Then Danny walked in and grabbed my arm and jerked it to the right. The gun fired. The bullet went into the wall.

But there was no question that I had a serious case of depression and that it was related to my dad's death. What made everything more complicated for me was the reaction around the country. He was in the headlines of all the New York papers and every other paper I saw when I went into a gift shop or newsstand. There were stories about him on television, on TBS and the Cable News Network, every hour or half-hour.

One of the channels ran an end-of-the-year review in December 1995. I saw my father's face and heard his voice. I didn't feel happy or sad. It seemed unreal.

It should have been comforting that so many people were mourning the passing of Mickey Mantle, but my feelings were on a much simpler level. My father died, and I didn't get to say to him what I wanted to say. I wrote him a letter, but didn't get to read it to him. I dropped it in the coffin before the services, along with a picture of me and Marla and Marilyn, his "little Miss America."

The letter isn't the one that you saw at the start of this chapter; that one was a reflection three months after we lost him. The first letter said I hoped he had been proud of us, that we tried always not to hurt him, and I loved him.

One of the drawbacks to getting sober is that things become halfway clear to you. The mysteries don't seem so deep, the mistakes so irreversible. What I decided was, you don't need to dwell on the mysteries of life and death. My father spent his last conscious hours on the twelfth of August, 1995. I couldn't help but reflect: My daughter, Marilyn, was born on that day—the twelfth of November, 1993. My brother, Billy, died on that day—the twelfth of March, 1994.

Mistakes? I'm glad our family is finally so open about the problems we've had. I hope we can help other families take the hard steps. I don't think you can afford to be shy when you have a name and you have a chance to share. You can't hide and act as if nothing was ever wrong.

Another thing being sober does, it causes you to do a lot of pondering. That's a heavyweight word. In the past, it was an effort for me just to think. Now I ponder.

In 1987, I had been living in Florida and hadn't seen my dad in nearly a year. I joined my brothers at one of our fantasy camps—the Mickey Mantle Week of Dreams—at Orlando. When I first saw him, Dad gave me one of those big smiles, shook my hand, and hugged me. Most people are not taken aback if they are greeted in this fashion by a desk clerk. I can't explain how very special it was.

I've had strangers tell me over the years how terrific it must feel to be the son of a celebrity. I wonder what it must be like to have a father who is available most of your life, instead of being gone most of the time. And you really get to know him in the last year and a half of his life, after you both have been sober.

I'm proud of his achievements in baseball. But it would have been nice to have been able to do the ordinary things we wanted to do as father and sons. And not have to be sheltered the way we were, or worry about what we said, how we dressed, what we looked like.

I had feelings of guilt about not serving in the military during the war in Vietnam. I registered for the draft at seventeen and that was the year they suspended it. I intended to enlist in the Marines, and a recruiter came by the house two days in a row to give me the tests and persuade me to join. When he said something about "being the one who recruited Mickey Mantle's kid," it just totally turned me off. I ended up not joining any branch of service. The discipline would have been good for me, but I let that little incident stop me and I shouldn't have.

We have two messages to deliver now, through the Mickey Mantle Foundation. One is being sober and the other is the critical need for organ donation. I am still amazed that the Betty Ford clinic has given our family a unified way of life. Those last eighteen months with Dad, all of us getting sober, were really unforgettable. I'm making public appearances around the country and I couldn't do them if I weren't sober. I'm getting better, but I have to ask people to be patient with me. I'm learning on the run.

In a way I feel as if I'm taking over one of Dad's roles. I don't know if Danny and Mickey feel the same way. But it isn't anything I'm forcing. When I speak in public, I sense that he is inside me and I'm acting the way he would act. I guess I'm trying to grow up and be the way he would want us to be—reaching out to people, getting them involved.

I don't kid myself that we can replace him, or that the crowds react to us in the same way. Being who Dad was, he was on an equal footing with other celebrities. I have to remind myself not to drop names or get carried away, because he disliked that whole scene.

But being his son I got to meet people like Muhammad Ali, who was probably the most famous athlete in the world. I got to work out with the fine actor Ben Gazzara, who stopped by the baseball camp one year to say hello to Dad. Once, Ted Turner jumped out of his box seat in Atlanta and came on the field to meet Dad before an Old Timer's game. This was what I had seen and heard all my life; that he had an aura, people were drawn to him, they wanted to meet The Mick . . . Number 7.

Instead of making too much of it, I think we may have gotten jaded. Junior and I had a chance to meet Elvis Presley one night in Las Vegas. Some press agent set it up: Dad had been the king of swing in baseball and he was going to pose with the king of rock 'n' roll. We blew it off and I still regret that we were too dumb to take advantage of a nice situation.

Growing up in the sixties and seventies, we all loved music and going to the concerts and reunions. My favorite group was Jethro Tull, and Dad was on a plane with them flying to Dallas and I had tickets to see them that night.

He was sitting next to Ian Anderson, who wrote most of their hits, including "War Child" and "Skating Away on the Thin Ice of the New Day." He said Anderson looked white as a ghost. But that is how the British are. They don't look as if they ever see any sunshine. But I couldn't get over it; my dad on the same plane as my favorite group and in a few hours I was going to see them in concert.

In the early eighties, the group INXS walked into a McDonald's in Joplin where I was working, on their way to

Kansas City. We were right off the highway. They were big then, but I didn't say anything to them. I didn't want to hound them or make a scene. Dad had always drummed that into us. When he was working at the Claridge Hotel in Atlantic City, Charlie Daniels was singing there. Danny and I asked him to introduce us. We kept bugging him and finally he said, "Okay, dammit, but don't you ever ask anybody for an autograph."

The last weekend in December 1995, we were in Atlanta to attend the world premiere of *Free Bird*, the movie about Lynyrd Skynyrd. Their plane crashed on October 20, 1977, the day my father turned forty-six. I heard the news of the crash and the deaths of Ronnie Van Zant, their lead singer, and the guitarist Steve Gaines. I felt kind of empty and depressed and those feelings returned when I saw the movie.

So that was what I was doing in Atlanta, and Charlie Daniels was there to perform at a concert in memory of the group. Charlie said that Dad called him from the hospital a week or so before he passed away. He had just heard about a song Charlie had written, in which he mentioned Mickey Mantle and John Wayne. Dad said, "Why did you have to stick John Wayne in there, too?" So Charlie said, "Well, Mick, who else would you have me mention?"

He said, "Nobody. Just me." That was his sense of humor, and he kept it right to the end. One reason I always liked certain musical groups was because they reminded me of the way it was when Dad played ball. They were all close, took care of each other and got into trouble together.

Another musician Dad met and got to talking with on a plane was Alice Cooper. I figured his long hair and makeup would freak Dad out, but he said Alice was a very intelligent guy and he really liked him. Alice straightened up his life, too, as many of the sixties groups have. He left all the crap in the past and got sober.

Among my memorabilia, I have a few pictures of Dad with his friends and teammates. But he was never a camera bug and didn't much like posing for pictures. I did a TV segment on fishing for ESPN once, with the former LSU and Baltimore Colts quarterback Bert Jones. The producers requested a still photo of me with my dad. I looked through all my photographs, several hundred, and couldn't find one that was of just the two of us, father and son. Not a single one. Isn't that a kick in the ass? I didn't ask him because I was worried what he would think. Now I don't have even one.

I don't know if my working at a McDonald's will seem out of character, but none of us were bums or playboys. I always worked. In Joplin, I was an assistant manager. The owner was a millionaire with a chain of five or six locations. I started at $10,400, worked for him almost three years, and when I left my salary was $12,000 a year. I was thirty years old, working every weekend and eighty hours a week, and the pay was a pittance. It's just a good thing I wasn't doing drugs then. Mom thought I was, but I couldn't afford it on my salary.

Long ago I fell into some of my dad's habits. He would tell me that I was loyal to a fault, that I tried too hard to make everybody happy. But that was the way I saw him. I wished that he had worked more on making himself happy. I wish he had liked himself more.

It's odd what different impressions the members of the

family have about Christmas. Danny thinks it was a sad, almost grim time for Dad. My memories of Christmas are mellow ones. He enjoyed acting like a little kid. He would put on all the old Christmas songs, and we'd sit around and watch the old movies on television, like *Miracle on 34th Street*, and Jimmy Stewart in *It's a Wonderful Life*. He would get very sentimental, I thought. Maybe he was happy giving us what he didn't have as a small boy.

Of course, his eggnog was notorious. It was so strong it could peel the silver off a spoon. But once you got the first one down, it was pretty tasty. The one thing that troubled me was the way he would take off the morning after Christmas, the 26th, which happened to be my birthday. That always bummed me out. His last Christmas with us was also the first year I could remember that he stayed home for my birthday . . . if he actually knew. He had a hard time keeping track of everybody's birthdays. Sometimes Mom would have my party a week early so he could be with me. But he never seemed sure what we were celebrating.

He blamed himself because each of his sons had a drinking problem and sort of floundered as adults. We had a wild, crazy streak and no doubt about it, we went through a stage where we must have thought we were Wyatt Earp and his brothers, reenacting the shootout at the OK Corral. That just grew out of the way we stuck up for each other. I may have been the chief offender. I daydreamed a lot and had a hero complex. I wanted to save people from burning buildings.

But there were some reckless and violent times, I can't deny it. Once some idiot tried to shoot Danny in the back with a shotgun. He missed and shot one of Danny's friends in the back by mistake. Then he whipped out a .38 and missed again, and this time he shot Danny's friend in the leg. (It wasn't easy being a friend of the Mantles.)

The word got back to Billy and me that Danny had been hit. I guess we were pretty wasted at the time, but we got our twelve-gauge automatic shotguns and went to a girl's apartment where this guy was supposed to be staying. We blew the door off the hinges.

There were a bunch of people inside partying, and we just started banging them around. I remember telling Billy, "If anybody moves, shoot 'em." I'm surprised and relieved that no one got shot. Keep in mind, we thought Danny had been plugged. Billy kept saying, "Let me just shoot one of them." Luckily, I had a little sense left and I said, "Naw, the guy we're looking for isn't here." Then we just left, walking over the door on our way out.

The guy who shot Danny's friend turned out to be a head case and a needle freak. The police were looking for him on another charge. When they found him, he started to wrestle with them and he got his hands on an officer's gun. When the cop got it back he shot him in the balls. So that was one vendetta we didn't have to handle.

We had gang fights in front of our house, even a couple of shootouts. I was still in high school, but nothing was organized. Usually they happened because somebody heard a rumor that turned out to be wrong.

We lived in a nice neighborhood. We just got crossways with some rough crowds. Our name was like a magnet. Guys just wanted to challenge us. Mickey Jr. never backed down from a fight, and I guess he had a reputation in our end of town as a badass. Danny and Billy always caught the brunt of things because they were younger and smaller. A carload of punks would drive by our house and try to taunt us. We made up our minds nobody was going to pick on us.

Dad's position was, don't go looking for trouble, but don't back down if somebody goes after you. We were glad he felt that way because one day there was a drive-by shooting, and they riddled Dad's brand new Buick Riviera with a twelve-gauge shotgun. There was so much gunplay in Dallas, even in what were thought of as upper-class neighborhoods, that the police didn't even come out to investigate it.

Once, when I lived in our house on Durango, I got a call from someone who threatened to come over and kill me. He said I was dating his former girlfriend. I didn't know who it was, so I called Mickey Jr., and he came over with a couple of his friends. We had a couple guys crouched behind the bushes and four or five of us inside the house and guns were everywhere.

The lights were down, the curtains closed, and we're peering out the windows. It must have looked like the Dillinger gang was hiding out. And stumbling up the front walk, here comes Dad. He takes a few steps, stops, studies the house, and yells out, "Hey, y'all, it's me. Don't shoot. What the hell is going on in there?"

It wasn't a laughing matter then, or today, when we know how dangerous that nonsense is. But the Mantle brothers took care of each other.

I'm not making up any of this. Dad didn't seem alarmed because he was gone so much, he only learned about a fraction of the rough stuff. When we told him our side, we were always in the right. I really believe we were.

We had outgrown most of the war games by the time we started to travel with Dad to his card shows. He was drinking a lot then, and disturbed by the early signs of memory loss. We made sure one of us would always be with him. We made sure no one took advantage of him when he was drunk.

He walked around like a lost puppy, wondering half the time what he was doing there. We all had separate rooms and there was always a block on Dad's phone. So Mom would call one of us if she needed to talk with him. We were not very good at lying to Mom when she asked if anyone was with him, but it didn't seem to matter. She usually knew the answer before she asked. We all played our parts.

He was lonely after Billy Martin died, and he no longer was able to see Whitey or his other buddies as much. A reporter asked him who his best friends were now and he said, "My sons."

When one or two of us stayed home, someone tried to sabotage us and turn him against us by feeding him stories. I suspect the woman he was seeing, but that may be unfair. He called Danny once from out of town and said, "What are you doing? I hear you're selling my bats."

Danny said, "Dad, what bats could you mean? If we were selling any, you'd have to sign them first."

There was another rumor that we were selling off his trophies. Those were all at Mom's house, except for the ones he had given away. It upset us bitterly that someone was messing with his head.

Junior traveled with him first, but then felt that he had put in his time and wanted to cut back. When Dad moved in with Danny, I was living in Florida, and Danny took his turn. When I moved back, I was eager to volunteer. I said, "Dad, I'd like to go with you now and then."

The first trip he ever took me on was to New York for several days in late 1990, the first time I had been back since he was inducted into the Hall of Fame in 1974. Kay and Danny had gone to bed, leaving Dad and me having drinks in the restaurant. His mood changed in a finger-snap. He broke down and started to cry. I looked at him and said, "Hey, Dad, what's wrong?"

He said, "I wasn't the kind of father you guys needed."

That was stale stuff and we had all gone beyond it. "Dad," I said, "we're okay now. That's in the past. I still love you. Don't be so hard on yourself. We've got lots of time now to make up for it."

But he kept repeating himself. "I wasn't there for y'all. I wasn't around."

He was feeling guilty and needed to say it. He didn't spare himself. We were all touched when he was interviewed by Roy Firestone on ESPN and he said, "When I think of what I did to my sons . . ." and he couldn't finish the sentence. It was a huge burden to him when his short-comings as a parent, as he saw them, sank in.

Of course, the guilt he carried over Billy would have bent the back of a camel. But he tried many times in many ways to show him how much he cared.

Mickey and Dad played in a golf tournament in Oklahoma City and Dad hit a hole in one, which was incredible, and he won a red Ford Mustang. He and Junior drove it all the way back to Dallas so he could give it to Billy.

Unfortunately, it was after midnight when they pulled in and Billy was pie-eyed drunk. Dad showed him the car, then told him to go back to his room and sleep it off. Danny and I were outside talking and suddenly Billy was in the doorway, arguing with Dad, who said, "Billy, you're not going anywhere."

Without a word, Billy headed for the car and got behind the wheel. Dad just opened the door and jerked him out and shook him a little. Billy kept trying to get back in the car, so we all gathered around and gave him a chorus of, "Billy, you're in no condition to drive."

Finally, Dad just picked him up and carried him inside the house and dropped him on his bed.

Billy was a little bulldog who never tired of seeing how far he could push Dad. We never had any sibling rivalries. I loved it when my father bragged on my brothers. When I was in high school, I got more than my share because I was the only one with a job. When I was thirteen, I worked at the restaurant, Mickey Mantle's Country Cookin'. To let me know I wasn't going to be treated like a spoiled brat, Dad had me scrub out the dumpster. When I finished, they filled it up again with all the garbage.

I went to college and got into a fraternity. I loved my brothers and didn't want Dad to single me out to a point where they might resent me. I mean my birth brothers, of course, although I got along fine with the ones in my fraternity at Baylor. I once talked Dad into driving to Waco and giving a talk at the frat house. I can assure you he was a hero that night. He was also warm and funny and relaxed.

Later, he stopped by the apartment three of us shared. We only had one chair, and we had to sweep off the debris so he could sit down. He couldn't believe his eyes. I don't know when, if ever, the place had been cleaned, and the floor was littered with beer and soda cans, dirty clothes, towels, dishes, and old hamburger wrappers. I asked Dad if he wanted to stay overnight, and he laughed out loud. When he got out his car keys to leave, he paused at the door, took one last look around, and shook his head. He must have been thinking, "If this is college, I didn't miss much."

Dad always had the ability to surprise you, at times when you expected the worst. I would get stressed out playing golf with him because he was always correcting me. I realize now he just wanted me to get better.

And I know he worried about me. He said I was the only golfer he ever knew who needed to wear a protective cup. I never knew where the ball was going. Once, he was sitting in the cart, with his back turned. My drive just veered to the right, hit him in the head, and knocked him out of the cart. He thought that was pretty funny.

He made allowances for me because he knew I was accident-prone. When I worked as a short-order cook, or even in our own kitchen, I kept nicking myself, cutting a finger or two. Dad said I probably should wear a protective cup in the kitchen, too, just in case.

At the fantasy camps, he really didn't want me to be the catcher because he was afraid I might get hurt. But one day we were short-handed, and I put on the mask and chest protector. They had a real tall umpire working the game, and when Dad came out of the clubhouse he couldn't get a clear look at home plate. "Who's that catching?" he asked.

Somebody said, "It's your son."

"Who, Mickey?"

"No, David."

And he said, "Oh, my God, get him out of there before he injures himself." About then, the batter hit a pop-up behind home plate and I lunged for it. The tall umpire gave ground to get out of my way, and I ended up sliding between his legs and missing the ball. It must have looked like a comedy act.

When I caught, I had a bad habit of holding out the mitt and turning my face. Dad pointed out that if I didn't flinch and kept my head straight, the mask would protect me. When I turned, the whole side of my head was exposed.

At one camp, I thought I was going to really catch hell. Dad had a touch of flu and went to bed early one night. My room was next to his, and his bed was against my wall. I went out and left the TV on, with the volume way up. That was a trick I learned from him. If you leave your TV on real loud, usually people will think you have company and not bother you.

He wasn't feeling well, couldn't sleep, and my TV sure didn't help. He called the desk and asked who the jerk was in the next room. I dressed quickly and headed out to the field the next morning, but when I looked up he was making a beeline for me in his golf cart. But he didn't yell. All he said was, "Why didn't you turn the TV down last night?"

I had to admit that I didn't realize how loud it was until I came in at four in the morning. When I got back to the hotel, my belongings had been moved to another room.

There were days when it was bliss to be Mickey Mantle's kid. Once, Dad and I were golfing partners against Mickey Jr. and a friend of his called Smooth. On the eighteenth hole, Dad and I were down $397 apiece. I had a tendency to get lucky on tough shots and miss the easy ones. We had a chance to pull out the match, if I could sink a really hellacious putt.

I had to push the ball uphill about fifteen feet, then have it stop and roll back down into the hole. I don't know how, but I did exactly what I had to do. The ball stopped right where it was supposed to, came back down the hill, and went straight into the cup. Junior was so upset he threw the flag in the air.

That putt saved us from having to pay them almost four hundred dollars each. Dad was so elated, he signed my scorecard with this message: "You could get Jack Nicklaus or any pro you want, give them a hundred tries, and none of them would make that putt." I think it was the surprise, not the money, that caused him to get a little carried away.

A friend of his, Bill Hooton, tells a story about asking Dad to join him for a foursome at Preston Trail that included Roger Clemens, the Boston Red Sox pitcher and one of my favorites. Dad had just gotten in and said he was tired and not sure he could make it. But the next day he joined them, was sort of quiet at first, then loosened up as the game wore on.

Hooton said that in the car, taking Clemens back to his hotel, Roger kept saying, "That was Mickey Mantle. Do you know who that was? That was Mickey Mantle!"

It's an odd feeling to root for a player and then find out my father was his idol.

When we were younger, he never wanted to give us a spanking, but we usually deserved one and he had to do it. Once I drove a go-cart through the sliding glass door of the trophy room. Another time I got mad and slammed the playroom door, and it knocked a silver trophy plate off the shelf in the room next to where he was watching television.

He was recovering from knee surgery, and I could hear him skip-hopping toward the living room so he could spank me. I just kept running around the couch and he kept chasing me. When I think about it now, I see it as a cartoon. He couldn't catch me and he kept telling me to stop, or he was going to whip me even more. He finally gave up.

He hated to lay a hand on us and he wouldn't tolerate anyone else doing it. I never understood what I did to upset her, but Dad's mother, Lovell, was always mean to me. She used to chase me around and hit me with a broomstick. Maybe it was because I was so hyper.

One day I was sitting on a stool in her kitchen, and I did something a kid would do. Dad told me she just backhanded me and knocked me off the stool. After that, he never let her watch me anymore because it really hurt him that she would give me that kind of swat. He said she used to whip him, too, something he didn't like to admit.

She was still Dad's mother and I respected her, but I didn't have the love for her that I did for Mom's folks.

I don't remember Dad raising his voice or getting mad at us. But as the years passed, when the alcohol got worse, he started to get verbally abusive. We would bust our butts to please him, and we couldn't seem to do anything right. He started to get belligerent and mean in 1992, and call us hyphenated names. There was nothing to mark that time frame except that the booze was taking its toll, the stomach pains were increasing, and his knees were always hurting.

It was hard to accept that it was the booze talking because we had soaked up a fair amount of alcohol ourselves. It hadn't yet turned us into gutter mouths. No matter what he might say, he would still give you the shirt off his back. Sometimes he would remember what he said and sometimes we couldn't tell if he did or not. That was his way of saying he was sorry, by not mentioning what had happened the previous night.

A lot of people can't say those words, "I'm sorry," so they act twice as nice the next day. If I was upset, I wouldn't call him and I usually called every day. So he would ask Danny, "Is David mad at me or something? What did I do now?" I would end up calling him back.

Once he called my wife, Marla, and broke the ice through her. They got along pretty well. She was always honest with him. If he asked a question, she told him exactly what she thought. If it was plain and blunt and he looked kind of surprised, Marla would say, "If you didn't want to hear the truth you shouldn't have asked me."

He would get into situations and not know where he was. He would call from a phone booth and ask Mom or Danny or me, "Help me. I'm lost. Come get me." But he couldn't tell us how to find him. It would take some detective work. Was there a store, a gas station, a sign nearby? Was there anyone he could ask? We always found him.

There were times when he locked himself in his room, not to keep anyone out, but to keep himself in. He didn't want to lose control and go wandering like some lost soul through the streets. Or get in the car and maybe hurt somebody.

We got into it one night at Jaxx, one of our favorite

Dallas bars. I took his car keys and wouldn't give them back. He called me one of those hyphenated names and said, "Listen, David, I am going to hit you if you don't give them to me."

I said, "Dad, you don't need to drive. One of us will drive you."

He said, "I'm going to take those keys. And I'm not going to tell you again."

I said, "Okay, then, take them." I handed him the keys. From the look in his eye that night, I think he would have hit me. If he had, I don't know what would have happened; if I would ever have forgiven him, or if he would have forgiven himself.

The same thing happened with Mickey Jr. It was Junior's birthday, April 12, and Dad almost caught us doing cocaine with a bunch of friends. We had the security chain across the door, and he said, "Don't you ever put the chain on to keep me out!" We were all at my house, and he turned to my friends and said, "All of you, leave the room." They got the hell out of there, scared of what might happen. They went to the back bedroom and didn't come out until he left.

I had a metal fan going full blast and he just reached up with his hand and stopped it. I don't know how he kept from slicing his hand off, but that's how great his reflexes were, even then. I said, "Dad, can I turn it off?" I walked a few feet and flipped the switch.

He lined us up against one wall, ripped off his sweater, and said, "Okay, y'all think you can take me, you think you can kick my ass, come on . . . "

We all said, "We don't want to fight you, Dad." He

grabbed Billy and then he grabbed me and gave us a little push. We kept saying, "Dad, we don't want to fight you. We love you." Then Mom came into the room to see what was happening and he sort of brushed her aside. Junior said, "Hey, Dad, don't push Mom. None of us want to fight you. We're not here for that. But don't take it out on her."

Then he grabbed Junior, who is so much like him that the effect was the same as one of those split images in a movie. Junior just gave him the cold fisheye and said, "Go ahead, hit me. But I'm not going to hit you back." Dad calmed down then, and after a few minutes he left. I called out to my friends, "You can come out now, he's gone." They just huddled there in the back room, in the dark, not even bothering to turn the light on. We sat around and laughed about it later, but at first we were scared and a little embarrassed.

His health was failing and no one knew it, including him. He just wasn't happy anymore, and it didn't take much to offend or upset him. His nerves were rubbed raw just before he stopped drinking. After an appearance, his first questions were, "Did I do okay? Did I make everybody happy? Was anybody mad?"

After being in treatment, I know now that he was depressed. I've had a bout of it myself, and you get irritable and tense and take it out on the people around you. After all the years of drinking, he was just lashing out. The fun in life had all but vanished for him.

When I think about those clashes, and where all of us were at one time, it tells me one thing: If families like ours can get sober, any family can. I checked myself into the Betty Ford Center because of Dad and because I didn't want to embarrass myself anymore. Danny and I were interviewed on television in New York after he got sober, and all the questions were directed at Dan. I was proud of my baby brother, and I knew I had to get straight.

It worked for all of us. You get a whole new outlook when you go into recovery. You think you are the only one with problems until you get out there. I heard some really gut-churning stories. You feel so bad for these people, and at the same time you begin to be convinced that you can deal with it. The eighteen months we had together when Dad was sober and we were all getting there was a blissful time. We didn't know that was all we'd have.

In the month after he went into the hospital, in late May of 1995, he suddenly got old. It was like the movie *Lost Horizon,* where the beautiful girl left the hidden city and suddenly was hundreds of years old. The cancer just shriveled him up, and the surgery, the chemo, the medication, all sapped his strength and aged a face that once seemed eternally young.

I find myself thinking about how quickly he was gone, the different stages he went through at the hospital. When he first went in, he was wearing pajamas and a robe, sitting up, talking and visiting, relaxed and optimistic. Then he was out of the pajamas and into one of those hospital gowns. Near the end you sat there, and he couldn't even watch television, really, because the morphine was dripping into his veins and he was listless, when he wasn't unconscious. You just held his hand and waited.

I resented the criticism he got from people who thought he had gone to the head of the list for a liver transplant. I know families feel helpless about their own loved ones. But he didn't get any special treatment. That was the way the protocol went: there's body tissue, blood type, size of the organ, all kinds of things involved.

His death didn't mean that a healthy liver was wasted. His death meant that millions of people were now aware of the organ donor program, who had no previous knowledge or interest. I can guarantee you this: My dad would rather have died than accept something he got unfairly.

I have thought about trying to define what a hero is. Dad was one throughout his baseball career, and a different kind at the end of his life. He was a man who learned from his mistakes, acknowledged his wrongs on television, and to the nation. Did Babe Ruth ever have to do that? He came to accept Christ. He gave himself to his family and friends and fans, and never really asked for anything in return.

I've had two heroes in my life, my dad and my mother. She didn't take it out on us because we protected him. He was always telling us to take care of Mom, and she wanted us to keep him out of trouble. So we knew they loved and cared about each other.

But I don't know if you can really explain why he was the object of such an undying love and sentiment on the part of guys in their forties, fifties, and sixties who were still in awe of him. He had a lasting effect on his generation and the one behind it, just coming of age. A lot of it was his looks, the fact that he played injured, the raw talent. But, also, he was nice to people when it wasn't easy for him. When he was rude, a lot of the time he couldn't help it. The fans clawed at him, tore his clothes, splattered ink on him trying to get his autograph. In crowds, he lost the ability to be loose. He lost the very thing they loved when he came to New York from the sticks—his freedom to be normal.

When Dad passed away, I didn't feel that I really had a chance to mourn. We were making plans for the foundation, and I wrote a lot of thank-you letters: to President and Mrs. Ford, and to Dad's old teammates, and to the friends who gave us support, including the Harley chapter that I'm in. I've been a motorcycle nut most of my life; I love the wind and the open road. My passion for Harleys was like his passion for putting on pinstripes. That was another thing Dad didn't understand about me, but I finally learned that was okay. Not everything is meant to be understood.

So I tried to get that across in one of my poems, one month to the day after he died:

I know now why he liked to sit up in his bed,
He would look out the window and marvel
at what he was thinking of in his head.
He went back to a time that had passed him by,
It was the days of his youth, a boy running
with his dog or a son with his dad,
this was the simple truth,
Probably thinking of his family as he grew up
learning to play ball was all he did.
This took his mind off the problems at hand
standing there, looking at this man,
knowing that there was no saving plan
which made it hard to understand
as I held my dad's hand,
like he did mine on my day of birth
with a desire and thirst to stay alive
and beat this curse.
I hope he knows how much I really love and miss him.

Chapter 8

Danny

There is a touch of Irish in Danny, from some forgotten limb of
our family tree. There is the gleam in his eye, and the kind of
charm you see in men who have a bottle of wine under each arm
and ring the doorbell with their elbows. Except now the bottles
are mineral water. As the youngest son, he inherited all our weaknesses, but he outgrew them. Danny is a late bloomer, maybe the
most stable among us, the one you trust not to lose the key to the
safety deposit box. He has a young son who is breaking him in. I
think he is going to be a terrific father.

—*MERLYN*

WHEN THE DOCTORS KNEW MY DAD'S CONDITION
was hopeless, he asked them not to tell him how
long he had left. I'm sure he had no idea that time
was so short. My wife, Kay, was expecting our first child, a
son, and up to a point his curiosity got the better of him.

We had decided to name the boy William, after Billy, and Charles, after Dad's middle name.

"I just hope I can get to see Will," he said to Dr. Goran Klintmalm. The due date we had then was December 2.

The doctor shook his head. That was all. Dad never mentioned it again, but I don't have any doubt how much that answer haunted him. His first son, Mickey Jr., had not lived to meet his grandfather. Now he was going to miss the birth of his first grandson.

Junior and David each had given him a granddaughter. We knew this one was a boy after Kay had undergone a sonogram. We could see his profile on the screen. It was weird. He looked like his daddy.

William Charles Mantle was born a few days early, on November 27, 1995. His grandpa had been dead for not quite four months. He was beautiful. He looked very much like his namesake, with dark hair and dark eyes and a little round face not much bigger than a baseball. He was a sweet-tempered baby. I loved holding him and couldn't take my eyes off him. Being a father made me realize how much I loved my father and how much he must have loved me.

From somewhere in the far recesses of my mind, I remember being at my grandparents' house in Oklahoma when I was three or four years old. I was sitting on Dad's lap and I think he said he loved me. I don't say this with any anger, but it was the only time I can recall him letting his affection show until I was well into my teens, seventeen or eighteen, and we had been out drinking. It was like the guy in the Bud Lite commercial who'd appear to be holding back tears as he blurted out the words, "I love ya, man." In our case, we would just order another round.

Until I reached the point where I could drink with him, I was always afraid of my dad—of Mickey Mantle. I can't really explain it. I was never physically afraid of him. He never hit us, although as we got older he threatened to take us on a time or two. This was when we would argue with him about who was sober enough to drive.

But this was a different kind of scared. He could give you a look that would scare the piss out of you. We were always creeping around, never knowing how he might react to anything, noise or bad news. All Mom had to say was, "I'm going to tell your father," and we straightened up pronto.

This phobia, if I can call it that, may have just gone back to the fact that we didn't know him. All our lives, we had heard about this guy the sports announcers talked about, but when he was home he either was at the golf course or out partying.

Each of his sons had a slightly different relationship with him and, in turn, we drew closer as we began to hang out with him. Except for Junior. He was always close to Dad. They played a lot of golf together, even when Junior was barely in his teens.

But none of this kept us from loving him. Good father, bad father, we never thought in those terms. I didn't realize how famous he was until after he retired, when I was eight. The only game I actually remember seeing him play in, he hit home runs back to back. I saw him run around the bases, heard the crowd screaming his name, and that was a thrill for me.

Even then I knew he was famous, but I didn't know what that was. His kind of famous caused people to imagine they were him in their dreams. Living in Dallas sheltered us from a lot of the Mantle mania.

I was born on March 19, 1960, the year Bill Mazeroski's homer beat the Yankees in the World Series. Dad had four or five good seasons left in him, but the last years were on mostly losing teams, and that had to be gnawing at him. I was a baby when we lived in New Jersey, when their long run of winning pennants was ending. To me, baseball was Florida, where in the spring we hung out with the kids of Whitey Ford and Yogi Berra and Phil Rizzuto. We had a blast. The Yankees were like an extended family.

Later, his fame embarrassed me. If one of my school friends started to tell someone who my father was, I'd give them an elbow and whisper, "Shut up. Don't tell anybody that." I didn't want to be seen as different from the other kids.

When I played Little League ball, I still felt the same mixed feelings. I was excited and proud when he came to a few of my games, but at the same time I felt I had to perform in some special way. If I didn't produce, I was lower than a sand crab, telling myself, Aw, I just can't do it. I'm not any good. Dad wasn't one to pass out words of encouragement. I don't think it dawned on him that I needed encouragement. He could probably see, even when I was eight or nine, that I wasn't going anywhere in sports. I don't really know what Dad's expectations of me were.

The sad part was, I felt relief when he didn't say anything. That was part of my being scared, and not wanting him to look at me in a disapproving way. I had a fear of failing that dogged me all through the growing-up years. I wouldn't take any risks, not in sports or in school. If I started something and was less than 100 percent at it, I would feel that I had failed, and I might disappoint Dad. Better not to start. I had no self-esteem, and in time that was probably the reason I drank so much. This was a family trend.

I think it's fair to say that Mom raised us. We got up, went to school, played after school like any kid would. We watched a lot of television. There wasn't a whole lot of what passed for family life—we didn't make a big deal out of birthdays. Holidays were usually spent intoxicated.

But all the brothers were close. We like our space, but we always stuck up for each other. We still do.

There wasn't a lot of pushing for us to achieve at anything. Dad didn't expect or demand much. I think I could have been a fairly good athlete, but I screwed up a knee in an accident in my teens. This and my fear of failing made quitting easier. At the fantasy camps, I always suited up and worked with the campers, but I felt like a misfit. I didn't have any speed and my knee would always give out. Dad would laugh or make jokes at the way I ran, and that was painful and embarrassing. I don't think Dad ever meant to hurt me by this. He never realized what it meant to me. He was just having fun, joking around.

But I need to make clear that I didn't start drinking because I felt neglected. I have learned to take responsibility for my alcoholism. I started drinking when I was about thirteen, on weekends with my friends from school. I remember the first time I actually got drunk. One of the guys got his older brother to buy us a bottle of wine, and we polished it off sitting in the middle of a football field.

But it would be foolish to say the family history didn't

figure into it. As a kid, one of the few contacts I had with my father was when I poured beers for him while he watched the football games on television. Even after he stopped playing ball he was gone a lot, and we'd go months at a time without talking. I can't remember carrying on a real conversation with him until I was seventeen.

When he was at home, the place had a way of filling up with people. We had touch football games in the back yard, with Dad's brothers and some of the neighborhood kids taking part, but, again, I was scared because I didn't want to mess up.

It was just like Dad always said: We didn't get close until we were old enough to be his drinking buddies. It reminded him of the old days with Billy and Whitey. That was how we connected; alcohol was the only way we knew how to open up. It wasn't until Dad was sick in the hospital that I could tell him that I loved him.

I have to admit, I wasn't aware until my late teens of the problems between Mom and Dad. I would see her crying sometimes at night, but I thought it was because he was gone so much. In my teen years, my dad didn't keep his affairs with other women a secret from my brothers and me. But I never sensed the pain my mother was feeling through this. I guess I felt what she didn't know didn't hurt her. I realize now she had to have known what was going on, and she had no one to confide in.

I never heard him raise his voice to her, but she had to be lonely as hell, a sentry in this camp of aimless boys.

I made it through high school, passing all my courses, but lacking any real drive. David attended Baylor for three years. I went to Brookhaven Junior College for about a year, to study television production. Due to my lifestyle, all the partying, this was one of those times when I decided I didn't want to cut it.

When I became a steady drinker, I still didn't think there was anything wrong. It was just part of having a good time. When you got to go out with Dad and Billy Martin, that was a blast. It was a way of getting to know him, and everyone always made a fuss over him.

I guess we all edit our childhood memories to some extent. I had a lot of good memories, but also a lot of painful ones. I left home when I was seventeen and moved in with a girl. I never liked going back to the house where we grew up. I had good memories with my brothers, but not as a family unit. When I was small, I shared Junior's room, and later I roomed with Billy.

When I was in treatment, they asked you to close your eyes and imagine different scenes in your life. When I thought of the house, it made me sad. When I was on my own and the rest of the family left town, Mom would ask me to watch the house. I'd always ask, "Can't you get someone else to do that?" The house had become a symbol of all that had gone wrong.

Of course, at seventeen, I wasn't entirely on my own. Mom paid my rent. As young as I was, with my own place and no goals, there wasn't much to do except drink. We all had a trust fund set up for college, but no one used it for that purpose. So money was never a problem. I probably had $20,000 in the bank, and I'd take out a hundred and fifty if I was going to party.

When I was twenty-eight, I began to realize that I was doing the same things I had been doing at seventeen—

drinking, staying out all night, doing some cocaine. I had jobs here and there, but none that I liked, nothing that ever lasted more than two or three months. David sold and serviced air conditioners for a while, and at one point I worked for him. I'd come in late or not show up. It was like, He's my brother, I don't have to treat it like a real job. I quit on him and left him in a bind.

I went to work for an oil company and held other odd jobs. But I never had any goal. Dad didn't seem to mind. He never paid a lot of attention to what we were doing with our lives.

When we started helping him with the card shows, the money was better than ever. David and I pooled our funds and opened our own shop in the Prestonwood Mall. It didn't seem to please Dad that we were trying to step out on our own. He may have been upset that we didn't ask him to bankroll us. When he was in town, he would call and say, "Close up and let's go do something."

"Dad," I'd remind him, "we're in a shopping mall. We have customers. We can't just close up."

He'd say, "Aw, bullshit."

When he wanted your company, or your loyalty, he wanted it at the moment he asked for it. For example, he woke me up one night after he came home from the funeral of Roger Maris. It was midnight, he was drunk, and he wanted to drive to Joplin.

I was still hung over from the party the night before, and the last thing on my mind was sitting in a car for six or seven hours. So finally he said, "Screw you. I'm going to load the damned car and go by myself."

I couldn't let him go alone, so I packed a bag and slid

behind the wheel. We drank the whole way to Joplin. I was twenty-five years old and I couldn't say no to him. None of us could. We had a protective instinct about him and that was one of the conflicts. To us, he was this indestructible figure and yet we knew we had to take care of him.

We lied and covered up for him with Mom. After they separated, in 1988, I lived with Dad in a two-bedroom apartment. He always had girls, some of them not a whole lot older than I was. He took me on trips so it would look like I was with him, rather than someone else. I always felt a certain competition with him when we traveled together. I was always trying to pick up girls. It was like, Well, hell, I can do this, too. I thought if I turned up with a couple of good-looking girls, maybe he would think more of me. It became a macho thing.

In the meantime, he was always saying, "Don't tell Mom this . . . or that." I was always caught in the middle. If I don't tell her, and she finds out, I'm in trouble. If I do tell her, I'm in trouble. If she never found out, I would still carry the guilt of lying. But I did what Dad expected.

His drinking didn't seem out of control or even excessive to me, because I was doing it, too. When the three or four of us went out with Dad, at the end of the night we would have a $700 or $800 bar bill. It was like a contest because no one wanted to quit.

I was the first to decide to check into the Betty Ford Center, for a very basic reason. I was scared. I always thought I could quit, and when I found out I couldn't, I had no choice. My life and health were falling apart. I would try. I'd be sober for two days and think, "Hell, that deserves a party," and I'd drink for three days. I had earned a reward.

I had sent for information from the Betty Ford Center probably five times. For three or four years, I had been swearing I was going there. I had promised Kay I would do it in August 1993. Now it was October.

I flew to California with Dad on a trip for Upper Deck. I helped Dad the first day, and then a friend of mine drove in from Newport Beach. Louie and I ended up getting drunk and Dad never saw me again that week, or the month that followed. We got into an argument on the phone because I had ducked out on him. I drank for three or four days straight and got very sick and scared. I decided this was the best time. I knew if I went back to Dallas I'd never go.

I didn't know if I could do it. Not only are you scared stiff about seeking help, you don't know what to expect. I only knew that I had to do something. In the back of my mind, a big question rattled around: How am I going to stay sober when everybody else in Dallas is partying their asses off? But I had gotten to the point where I didn't want to die.

I was fed up with the type of life I was leading and even with letting my father run me. I thought, if I ever wanted to accomplish anything, if I ever wanted to have a family of my own and a decent job, I had to get my head straight. To begin with, there was no way I could do zilch in the shape I was in. I had saved some money. I hadn't asked anyone to pull any strings to get me into the Betty Ford Center. I did it on my own. Actually, I felt like this was the first time I had done anything without the help of Mom or Dad or anyone else.

The tuition was $12,000. Luckily, I carried my own insurance and that paid half. I put the other $6,000 on my

Visa card. Then I called and asked Kay to come out, and I wrote a check for her treatment.

Dad had no idea where I was. I was calling Kay from California in the middle of the night, really drunk, yelling and calling her names. Just that alcoholic behavior that was so familiar to all of us. Kay was packing her bags to leave when Dad walked into the house we were sharing and asked, "Where's Danny?"

She said, "I don't know where he is right this minute, but he's supposed to meet me in Palm Springs and we're going to check into the Betty Ford Center." He didn't really believe her. Kay wasn't sure to believe it herself. She had been hearing this story for years. She said later, "I thought, This is a nice try, but I'm not going to get my hopes up." She packed a bag for the weekend and left.

We made it. We got clean and finished our stays. Kay and I were both nervous about going home. I didn't know how to act because I knew that nothing around us had changed. But the reaction was great. The whole family was glad for us and proud.

We were especially concerned about how Dad would react to our sobriety. Dad never liked to drink alone, and because of our living situation, we felt we might get a lot of pressure to drink with him.

It turned out to be quite the opposite. Dad was so proud of what we had done, he literally told us all the time, especially when he had downed a few himself.

At dinner one night with Dad, he said, "Man, I wish I could do what you guys did." He had been drinking most of the day and now he started to cry, softly, so the other tables might not notice.

Kay and I told him, "Dad, you can do it."

"You really think I can?"

"Hell, yes, you can."

On January 7, 1994, he finally did. He kept asking us questions, so I knew the message was sinking in. I saw the process of his mind, the questions, the curiosity. What worried him most was having to open up to people. He asked his friend Pat Summerall if they harped on religion a lot. I think he just didn't want anyone preaching to him. He said, "I believe in God. I just don't go to church and sit around talking about it all the time."

As I think back, Dad's greatest fear was probably having to expose his true feelings, because that meant he would first have to decide what those feelings were. It would be especially hard for someone like him, who could envision everybody going home and telling their friends what Mickey Mantle had to say. I'm sure that stuck in the back of his mind.

The last year and a half of Dad's life, when we were all sober, we talked about so many things we would never have touched on in our liquid days. If he had a kind word for any of us, or just thanks, it meant something now because we were sober.

The people he accepted quickly and seemed to appreciate, in his own quiet way, were the ones who didn't need anything from him. Kay won his respect just by being herself.

"I didn't even know who he was," she tells people, "when I met Danny. I came from a large farming family, and I grew up with a hard work ethic and good morals, and on that level he related to me."

Danny

When she first moved in with me, we lived in the second bedroom in the apartment Dad had rented. He was still gone more than he was home. We had our privacy and, when he was around, most of the time we had fun.

One day, Dad asked Kay if she would iron a shirt for him. You knew two things from that: He must have been out of laundered shirts, and that one had to really need ironing. He wasn't the kind of person who would ask for anything. She ironed the shirt and he went to keep an appointment. That night, when Kay came home, she found a couple dozen Tyler roses all over the apartment.

Dad used to try to give her money, and he didn't fully understand why she would never accept it. He never knew how to show his feelings, so he used money as a tool to show gratitude or affection. But all she wanted was for him to realize she didn't expect money to do the things around the house that she did. She did those things because we were a family, we loved each other—and him. Kay called him Mick, and he called her his roomie.

We had some strange and comic turns along the way. I'll let Kay describe this one in her words.

"We were all drunk one night. We had been out partying and back at the house Danny and I got into a fight. I knew about Mick's other women and I worried about Danny. I didn't want to be suspicious every time he left town, but I knew how close they were now and I also knew the fruit doesn't fall far from the tree. I knew it was going on with Danny, too. That's what we were fighting about, but I had no proof.

"When Danny and Mick were on the road, there were times the phone calls would come in the middle of the

203

night, when I was at home alone, and Danny would ask me who was there with me at three o'clock in the morning. This was his guilty conscience talking. I knew that. So when we would go out to dinner, I'd flirt with other men because I didn't know how to get back at him. On this particular night, that was what started the argument and one of us tried to leave. The fight spilled into the yard and there was Mick, in his underwear, trying to break it up and get us back inside." We were all drunk. It was just that typical alcoholic behavior.

After he left Mom, Dad kept a one-bedroom townhouse in Dallas, but he was rarely there because he hated being alone. I was ending a relationship with a girl and when he was home, and we talked, I told him I wasn't doing so well. He jumped on the idea. "Well, hell," he said, "come over here and I'll get us a two-bedroom and you can live with me." So in 1989, I took him up on it. By then, we were drinking together and going out pretty regularly. The whole family liked the arrangement because it kept him at home more and now he had company. I enjoyed the arrangement because I never before had that closeness. I liked going out to eat with him every night. Of course, we would end up drinking.

He never lectured us because he knew he couldn't defend his own behavior. But once when Billy overdosed and was in the hospital on a respirator, none of us wanted to see him like that. Dad said, "You're going to see him." And we did. Nothing else needed to be said. It was right there in front of us: *See, look at Billy. That can happen to any of you.* I think he knew we were doing drugs, and he never had. He didn't understand the drug culture and never would. That really worried him.

As I said, each of the brothers had his own personality and his own role in Dad's life. David was funny, hyper, and offbeat. Junior was almost a clone of Dad, with that silent, aloof side to him. I fell somewhere in the middle. Billy, well, we loved Billy, but he was the black sheep, the one who kept getting in trouble. In Billy's later years, he was out of contact with most of the family, except for Mom.

In time, Dad turned to me, but not because I was "the sensible one." In 1989 and 1990, I was the only one who was single. Mickey and Cindy were still married. David and Marla were married. I was available. He expected me to do the traveling, to be there when he needed me. He started asking me for advice. I thought, Wow, shouldn't it be the other way around? We didn't have any secrets between us.

I didn't mind, not really, but it was as if I couldn't have any commitments except to him. Instinctively, Kay knew this and accepted it. But she really had no idea what she was getting into when she moved in with us in April 1989.

We were all drinking one night at the Atlantic Cafe, one of Dad's favorite places, and as we got into his Cadillac he started to feel sick. I got into the back seat so I could kind of cradle his head, and Kay had to drive, which was unusual and unsettling. Dad didn't like anyone else to drive and she was tipsy herself. She hit the curb backing out because she saw how ghastly Dad looked and she was half terrified.

The next morning, he didn't remember getting sick or even drunk. All he remembered was Kay hitting the curb. "Well," he told her, "that's the last time we let you drive." His memory had huge holes in it, but as Kay said, he had the ability to remember what he wanted to remember. And at the most surprising moments, he could be the only one in the room who was thinking clearly. Lord knows, don't ask me how.

Back when Billy Martin was managing the Yankees for the third time, in 1985, Dad went to see them play the Rangers. Later, a bunch of us met for drinks at the Hilton Hotel in Arlington, where the visiting team stayed. Then Dad and Billy Martin, a couple of his coaches, me, and Mickey Jr. piled into a car and drove to a strip joint in Arlington near the stadium. Dad could see the trouble coming. Some fans at the bar started heckling Billy, who as any serious baseball fan knew never backed off from a fight.

Dad leaned over and told Junior to take me home—I was twenty-five, but still the baby brother. Sure enough, after we left, three guys jumped Billy and damn near tore his ear off. Dad got out of there before they started knocking over the tables and throwing chairs, and he avoided being a part of the bad press.

He was so strong, he could certainly take care of himself. But he didn't like to hit people; even when his judgment was impaired he knew how to avoid a confrontation.

On another night at the Atlantic Cafe, we were having drinks—Kay and Junior and a friend of Junior's, Bill Durham, were there. We were about the only ones in there and the piano player was still tickling the ivories. I don't know if the music made him sad or hurt his ears or just made it harder to talk, but he had a thing about pianos.

Dad called over the waitress and said something like, "I'll give that guy a hundred bucks to quit playing."

After she relayed the offer, the guy at the piano looked up, smiled, and said, in a smartass tone of voice, "Oh, it seems the great Mickey Mantle doesn't want me to play anymore." And he did a few riffs on the keyboard for emphasis.

That ticked off Junior, who was trying to get up and squeeze his way out of the booth. He had ordered one of those coffee drinks with whipped cream on the top, and he had a white mustache. Dad thought he was foaming at the mouth, and he grabbed him and held him back. I had to tell Dad it was just whipped cream.

Some of the incidents had that kind of comic undertone, but a lot didn't. You often felt on edge when it was late at night in a bar and the drunks started to get louder. At any moment, you felt that somebody was going to challenge Mickey Mantle.

Dad was out of town the night five of us borrowed his new white Cadillac to go to a concert. I knew we shouldn't. The car had less than 2,000 miles on it. Sure enough, we wrecked it. David and Kay and a friend were in the back. I was in front with another friend, who was driving.

We were broadsided by a car that came speeding over a hill as we pulled out of the parking lot at a convenience store. I had a broken rib but it was David who was seriously hurt. No one realized at first how seriously. He had been whiplashed by the impact, struck his head against the rear window, and had blood all over him. They took him by ambulance to the hospital, where he was treated and released.

After a couple of days of suffering with a fierce headache and blurry vision, they had to check him back in.

He had fluid on the brain. They had to drill a hole in his skull to relieve the pressure and drained enough blood to fill a syringe.

Kay went back to the convenience store to call Roy True and ask the attendants to call 911. They didn't know how, so Kay made the call. Roy arrived just after the ambulance and before the police. In a coincidence that was almost eerie, Billy happened to drive by just minutes earlier, saw it was us, and stopped.

The first thing Roy said was, "Billy, what happened?"

Billy said, "Don't ask me, I was just passing by." Poor Billy was the only one there who had nothing to do with it.

The Caddy wasn't worth repairing. Injuries or not, no one who really knew Dad wanted to make him mad or bring him bad news. The next day, Roy True was flying to New York to meet him, and I pleaded with him to tell Dad for us.

Roy wasn't thrilled with the idea, either. But he came through, as he always did. He walked into Dad's hotel suite and almost the first thing he said was, "Well, Mick, what kind of new car do you want?"

Dad laughed out loud. "What the hell do you mean?" he asked. "I've got a brand-new car."

"Not anymore you don't," said Roy.

Not long after we started living together, Dad decided to build a new, larger house—the one Kay and I have today—and the three of us moved in. It wasn't a Grumpy Old Man thing. Dad and I were not an Odd Couple. We didn't have to divide the responsibilities. I had them all. At that stage, Dad was really an easygoing person. Two things upset him: When he would come home from a trip, he hated finding the smell of cigarette smoke in the house. And if we were out of Equal, Sanka, Evian water, half-and-half, or Frosted Flakes, it was the end of the civilized world as we knew it. This didn't happen often, but when it did you heard him.

At six o'clock the next morning, you'd hear the front door slam shut as he drove over to the nearest convenience store to stock up.

I sometimes wonder if the rest of the family would have gotten help if I had not made the decision to get into treatment. Mom was the only one to come out for family week. I had heard that if one person gets help the others will follow, but at that point I was more concerned about myself. They kept reconfirming this at Betty Ford—focus on your own problem. The truth is, I didn't think the others would come, least of all my dad.

When I returned he really wanted to get sober, but he felt handcuffed. A lot of what he was doing was appearing at cocktail parties and award dinners and he thought, "How would I get through that?" It was fear, and it was well founded. Every once in a while, I catch myself wishing I could have a cold beer.

We used to come back to the house after partying all night and dance. We would put on an Alan Jackson tape and crank it up as loud as it would go, and Dad would grab Kay and do his Fred Astaire imitation. With his wobbly knees, that was quite a sight. We would sit around for three or four hours, laughing and calling up people and waking them up.

The mischief maker in Mickey Mantle would come alive. He dreamed up a story in the wee hours one morning: He had me call David and tell him two guys he knew from Baylor had kidnapped Dad. We were knocking ourselves out laughing, when I called back to tell him it was a joke. Marla said David had raced out the door with a shotgun. She had to go running after him.

After he came out of the Betty Ford Center, Dad was a different person. He started to visit his mother, who was in a rest home in Oklahoma, and I'd go with him. I saw her more in the last three months of her life than I had in all the previous years. She died in March 1995, a year to the month after Billy's death.

Grandma Mantle was ninety-two, and Dad had gone years without visiting her. I think he disliked seeing her get old and feeble. But now he wanted to make up for not spending a little time with her. After he got sober, he took the time to do things he never would have done before.

When we were leaving her funeral and walking back to the car, Dad said to me and Kay, "I hope I'm next because I'm not going through this shit anymore." That was eerie. But it wasn't meant to be prophetic. He was tired of burying his friends and members of his family. He didn't want to sit through any more funerals. He had buried his father, his son, and his mother, and three or four of his closest teammates.

After Billy passed away, he really felt a sense of loss. We went to the cemetery on Billy's birthday and Dad just stood there and stared at the plot.

Dad liked being sober. It was amazing and sad and ironic. After forty years, he finally did something so difficult and so good for him, not knowing that he had only a few months to enjoy the new life he had discovered.

He started telling us more frequently that he was proud of us. All the boys were working at the card shows and fantasy camps. Even if you just hit a good drive on the golf course, he would pay you a compliment, which he rarely did in the past. A friend of his said something nice about me once and Dad said, "Yeah, I know. Everybody likes Danny and I can't figure it out." I'm not sure he was kidding. He wasn't analytical, and what made people tick was a subject that puzzled him.

I don't want to pretend that we didn't have a good time during the drinking days, because we did. We were best friends and hung out together and it was fun. But after he went into treatment the times changed, and for the better.

It was a kick to watch Dad trying to help with the dishes. And Kay bought him a plastic egg-poacher in the shape of a chicken that cackled when your eggs were ready. He loved it. He fixed his own eggs in the morning and acted as if he had invented the cotton gin. He took pride in the little family things we started doing together.

Mom used to joke about watching us drive away after dinner at a restaurant. Kay and I would be in the front seat, and Dad would be poking his head right between us from the back. We'd be laughing and talking—and this was when we were all sober. Mom said Kay and I looked like the parents, and Mick was the kid.

There was a closeness and warmth the three of us shared just watching TV and making bets on the baseball games. Mick always got to pick his team first. We'd even bet on the questions on *Wheel of Fortune*. Even if I wasn't there, Dad bet for me and I always lost. I'd walk in and he would say, "You weren't here, so you're fifty dollars in the hole." Of course, no one ever paid off, but it was our running joke. Kay can't watch *Wheel of Fortune* anymore.

Before he got sober, he didn't like to stay home and have dinner. He was too restless. He had his routine, going to one restaurant or another, ordering food he rarely touched while he drank the night away. But once we were all sober, he looked forward to eating at home. He would call from the club and ask Kay what we were having for dinner, and what time he needed to be there. He was never late.

He didn't always succeed, but all of his life he wanted to be reliable. To him that meant being punctual. He would chew me out for being five minutes late.

He lived with us the last six years, in the townhouse and then the one he had built with four bedrooms because we thought we were going to be together for a long time. He was relaxed in that house and he talked about things that had been buried inside him . . . what it was like when he was a little boy, how the family moved around, how they never had anything. How his father worked a farm, spent a year raising the crops that would pay their bills and buy some small comforts, and a flood washed it all away, the crops and the dreams.

Being poor, and living the way he did, left a complex in him that he never really overcame. Oh, he layered things over it, with the expensive clothes he wore and the fine material goods he learned to appreciate. He said it over and over: "My dad would be spinning in his grave if he knew how much I was making in a day for signing my name."

We talked about my regrets, too, the years I had wasted drinking. When we would be watching a college football game together and the camera panned the stands, it would hit me hard. I missed that. I missed not going to college. I missed out on a lot of the normal things people do when they grow up.

I really regret not getting a college degree because I might have done something worthwhile with the years I blew away. I didn't even try because the drinking steals your ambition. Also, when you stay out until three or four in the morning, you can't get your ass out of bed for a nine o'clock class.

Dad felt secure with Kay and me. Some nights, if we were getting ready to go out, he would say, "Oh, man . . . do you mind staying home tonight? I'm not feeling good."

He had many premonitions, but when he was really sick he would try not to let anyone know. He wasn't afraid of dying so much as he was afraid of what he didn't know. He would pepper us with questions: What do I do if I can't breathe? How do you call an ambulance? When he was in one of those moods, we couldn't leave him.

The time he hyperventilated on the plane, after being with Billy and Whitey at the fantasy camp, I stayed with him at the hospital. The panic attacks started to come with some regularity. He would go on a three- or four-day drunk, freak out, and then check into a hospital.

The idea of being helpless, being an invalid, being at the mercy of others, held real terror for him.

A day or so before his surgery, Dad mentioned a friend of his who claimed to have visits from his late wife. "Can you see Stella?" he would ask a friend. "She's right over there." Dad would walk away shaking his head and thinking, "Gee, old Harold is going nuts."

He told Junior, "You know how we used to laugh at Harold? Well, that shit's true. I saw Billy. He was just sitting on the dresser, with his hands at his side, palms down. We didn't talk. But it was him." Later, he said he saw Billy a second time.

Maybe you want something so bad, you can convince yourself it happened. All I know is, anyone who heard the intensity in Dad's voice would have had a hard time disbelieving him.

After the surgery, for a few fleeting days, we thought the prospects were good. He was going to get another turn at bat. He had a new liver and, in spite of the controversy that ensued, we were all upbeat. The latest CAT scan looked good. And we knew the truth: He hadn't skipped to the head of the organ transplant line because he was Mickey Mantle. He was the one who met the criteria. He was the one the organ matched, the nearest in proximity to the donor, and among the candidates most in need he was the sickest. Without it, the doctors gave him forty-eight hours to live.

When we brought him home, he was filled with plans to use the foundation to get behind the organ donor program. But he had lost forty pounds and needed to get his strength back. He was driving himself back and forth to the club and I'd meet him there. We would have a light lunch, and he would spend a few minutes on the treadmill and in the sauna. It wouldn't take long for him to run out of steam. We would go home and watch television.

He complained about the air conditioner being out on his Ford Explorer, a 1992 model. He kept telling me it had gone out, but every time I turned on the engine the air worked fine. Kay and I decided to surprise him with a new, dark green, 1995 Explorer. When we drove it home, parked it outside, and told him to come see his new car, his eyes just lit up. You could tell how tickled he was.

But he never got to drive it.

He started noticing the pains in his stomach and chest two weeks after he left the hospital. I think Dad knew something was terribly wrong. He stopped eating. He sat at the table and tried to put a bite of food in his mouth, and he couldn't do it. All he could get down was a can of Ensure, a drink used as a diet supplement. I told him, "Dad, that stuff isn't going to help." But he wasn't being stubborn. He hurt too much to eat.

Kay was four or five months pregnant, and she would be up at one or two o'clock in the morning, unable to sleep. She would lie on the couch trying to get comfortable. In a few minutes, Dad would come out of his bedroom. He had heard Kay moving around. He had such severe stomach cramps, he didn't know what to do. And he was scared.

Two weeks after he was released the first time, he went back to the hospital and they took a second CAT scan. I was in the room when two of the doctors told him how fast the cancer had spread. They hadn't yet given up hope and were planning to put him on the chemo.

As soon as the doctors left, he looked at me and said, "Don't tell anybody."

I said, "Dad, we got to tell somebody. This isn't like a cold or something."

He said, "Naw, I don't want anybody to know because I don't want anybody feeling sorry for me."

By late July, the last doubt was erased when Dr. DeLarios called Mickey Jr. and me down to his office. He showed us the X rays and this time the cancer was everywhere. One of us asked, "What does this mean?" The doctor said, "Ten days, two weeks, tops."

Mickey and I just looked at each other. The new liver was ravaged. The cancer had spread to his pancreas, his lungs, and the lining of his heart. Which proved what the doctors were saying—how aggressive it was.

I told Dr. DeLarios, "You have to tell him. I can't do it." So he went back to the room with us and told him exactly how bad it was. Dad broke in and said, "I'm not going to get better, right?"

The doctor said, "No, and in terms of time . . ."

Dad broke in and said, "Thank you." Then he shook his head and added, "I don't want to know."

He was heavily medicated, and one day he looked up at David and said, "Why are you making me wait?" But he would be lucid for periods of time. It was the middle of the season in baseball, and we watched the games on the TV set in his room. We watched the O. J. Simpson double murder trial. Dad became a faithful viewer; it beat all the soap operas. He didn't like F. Lee Bailey and he wasn't crazy about Marcia Clark. He predicted O. J. would be acquitted, but he thought he was guilty.

Toward the end, we were all nearly frantic trying to decide what were the right things to do and say. He didn't want anybody to see him hurting. He tried to go as long as he could without the pain medication, but the time between doses got shorter—four hours, then three. The last few days, one of us would push the button for him and release the morphine.

Once the doctor came in and said, "Try skipping a dose and see how it goes." The next thing you knew, he was in excruciating pain and the cycle started all over again.

He kept saying he didn't want anybody to see him, and he didn't want sympathy. It was hard for us, his sons, to see him the way he was. The once-muscular body was down to 140 pounds. His stomach was bloated and his legs were swollen. His skin was yellow. It was our decision to call his old Yankee teammates and tell them to come if they wanted.

Whitey and Bobby Richardson came first, the day before Hank Bauer, Moose Skowron, and Johnny Blanchard. As soon as I let Whitey into the room, Dad grinned and called me a hyphenated word—but he was kidding. He kept apologizing to them because he couldn't talk very easily. They said, Don't worry about it, Mick. We just wanted to see you and say hi.

I don't know where he found the strength, but he got up and made it over to a chair during their visits.

When he was lucid, I never knew how much time we had to say what needed to be said, or where to start. He asked me to make sure everybody lived right. I nodded. I wanted to tell him we were going to be fine, and we would always look after Mom, but I'm not sure how the words came out.

I don't expect to ever meet a prouder man. Two days before he died, he still refused to pee in a bottle. I don't mean for that to sound coarse or trivial. I had to help him back and forth to the bathroom. He had one of those walkers, with the bottles and the morphine connected to various tubes. It was like moving a pharmacy. He was in and out of the haze those last forty-eight hours.

I was back at the hospital in November. This time I was in the delivery room when my son Will was born. My first thoughts were of Dad. I wished he could see him. I was ecstatic, but at the same time part of me felt empty. We had wanted to ask him to autograph a ball for Will. Kay reminded me of it two days before he died.

Dad had joked about it so many times, the story of going to heaven and being turned away because of the life he had led on earth. "But before you go," St. Peter asked him, "would you mind signing a half-dozen boxes of base-balls for God?"

Now he was sick and dying, and I couldn't ask him to sign one more, not even for his first grandson.

Merlyn

Thousands will live because Mickey Mantle died. This is the truth of what happened in August 1995. This is the bottom line. This is what the doctors say and what I believe now and always.

Chapter 9

A Graceful Good-bye

OUR RELATIONSHIPS, MINE AND MICK'S, HIS WITH THE boys, had taken a gentle turn in the spring of 1995. I'm not sure that I could explain then what we had between us, and it isn't any easier now. We had grown closer, more thoughtful, more open, more relaxed than we had ever been. My husband had become my beloved friend.

When we went out to dinner, we went as a happier family. We touched. We laughed. Our friends saw it, and so did the owners and managers of the restaurants where in the past we had done more drinking than eating.

Mick was proud of all of us for what we had gone through, except himself. He was still too filled with regret to take any credit for getting sober.

David was the fourth member of the clan who had gotten into recovery. In September 1994, he had followed

Danny and Mick to the Betty Ford Center. I had done it my way. Mickey Jr., in his own good time, was sneaking up on it.

I was still getting used to the changes in Mick. They were startling. He always believed in God, but in his harsh way of thinking, he feared he would be a hypocrite if he went to church because he had not led a religious life. Now he had started going to a small nondenominational church that Danny and David and their wives had joined. He would sometimes wait until the services had started, then slip in the back door and take a seat in the last pew.

He would get excited talking about the charities he wanted to help, and becoming a spokesman for programs that warned kids against drugs and drinking. He was turning into the kind of person the fans, in their blind faith, always thought he was.

He was staying home more, with Danny and Kay. He even cleaned up his language. I began to believe that Mick could have a whole new life ahead of him, a rich and healthy one, and the family would be a part of it. But none of us realized at the time how ill he already was, and how short his period of grace would be. He left the clinic in February, endured two or three months of tension while his system adjusted, and felt really good from June of 1994 to the end of the year.

Then it started falling apart. Even though he was finding it harder to hide his pains, he kept putting off getting a complete checkup. We worried about him, but no more than we always had. We knew his knees were a constant hurt, and if his stomach acted up that was nothing new. We both had ulcers, and he had been operated on for a hernia.

But something was different. His skin was yellowish and he had self-diagnosed the pain in his abdomen as cramps, and his pockets were filled with antacid tablets. It didn't seem fair that he should be feeling so bad, now that he was sober and keeping respectable hours.

In May, Danny and Kay, who was pregnant, invited me to join them on a trip to South Dakota to visit her parents. Traveling by car was a concession to me and my fear of flying. I have always had this phobia. In the past, I dealt with it by having a couple of stiff drinks before I got on the plane, and whatever the limit was during the flight.

I know this condition is not uncommon, and for most of us the problem is the feeling of being trapped in a small space—acrophobia. The fear almost ended the careers of Jackie Jensen and Don Newcomb, among many baseball players, and it did hasten John Madden's decision to retire from coaching. Many people try to deal with it through hypnosis. Nothing really worked for me. I made many a trip across the country with four restless boys in the car, so there is really no reason I should fear anything.

Shortly before we left, Mick said he thought a few days of bed rest would cure whatever was ailing him. He had done this in the past after a long drinking binge, and usually bounced back. This time he would stay in bed for five days, and the pain would never leave.

The day before our trip was to start, David stopped by Danny's house to talk about their dad. David was upset enough over Mick's condition that he wanted to call Dr. DeLarios, his internist. Danny agreed.

David got him on the phone and said, "Dr. D., Dad isn't getting any better and he's just lying in bed and suffering. Maybe you can talk to him and get his butt in the hospital."

At that point, Dr. DeLarios confided that he had already arranged for Mick to be admitted to the Baylor University Medical Center for tests. But Mick wouldn't go until he knew that Danny had gotten me safely out of town. I think he sensed how sick he was and wanted to keep it from me, from all of us.

We left on a Saturday. The next morning, May 28, Mick called and asked David to drive him to the hospital. "When I went to pick him up," said David, "his bag was packed and he was sitting on the edge of the bed, kind of doubled over, in real bad pain and trying to conceal it. We didn't say much on the way to the hospital. I could tell he was worried and that got me worried.

"When I pulled up to the main entrance, I dropped him off and said, 'I'll park the car and go in with you.' Dad said, 'No, no. Don't worry about it. You go on. I'll be out probably tomorrow. They'll get a couple tests done and I'll call and you can pick me up, if not tomorrow, a couple days at the latest.' I could tell he didn't want me to go inside with him. He said Dr. DeLarios was meeting him in the admissions office."

David was reluctant to leave, but he said, "Okay, I'll call or come by tonight. If you need anything, let me know and I'll bring it with me."

He looked weak as David watched him walk away, and his body sagged. It was typical of Mick not to want us to worry, and to keep the gravity of his illness a secret as long as possible. I'm not sure what he would have done if I had not gone on the trip with Danny and Kay.

In the end, his pride and his need for privacy always took over. He might have found a hospital out of town and checked in.

Of course, that was what his own father had done nearly forty-five years earlier. He went to a clinic in Colorado, so his family wouldn't watch him waste away with cancer. Mutt Mantle died just five months after Mick and I were married.

David stopped by the hospital that night. They were not going to start the tests until the next morning. When David left, his dad called after him, "If you talk to her on the phone, don't say anything to your mother."

We had left the phone number of Kay's parents in South Dakota, in case he needed to reach us. He could not keep it from Danny that Mick was going to have the tests done. If the news was bad, David was to call us so we could come right home.

Mick had been in the hospital for a week and he was still telling David, "Don't worry Mom. Let them enjoy their trip. There's no reason to call them now and get them upset." But on Tuesday, June 6, his condition took a dive, and the doctors decided to put him on the list for a liver transplant.

Few outside the family knew he was ill or even in a hospital. Roy True and his office administrator, Kathy Hampton, knew. So did Murphy Martin, a former ABC newscaster and a friend of many years. When Mick was conscious and alert, he and Murphy played pinochle.

Roy was in the room when the doctors told Mick his liver was beyond healing. The tests had shown spots of cancer. He needed a new one. After they left, Mickey looked at his longtime friend and lawyer and said, "Well, it looks like I've done it this time."

There was an odd note of remorse and relief in his voice. One way or another, the scorebook was going to be balanced now and he might have been glad to have it out of his hands. For the wreckage of his health, he blamed no one except himself. In his own way, as penance, in the last year and a half he had tried to do all the right things.

There had been no announcement when he entered the hospital, but now it would be virtually impossible to keep quiet how critical his condition was. At Mickey's request, Roy True issued a statement that said he "regrets his lifestyle. He has said on many occasions that he hopes he will serve as an example to youngsters out there, who may think drinking is a lot of fun, a big blast, and that they will have second thoughts about it."

The bad news call from David came that day, and the three of us left the car in South Dakota and caught a plane back to Dallas. We saw him late that night, in intensive care. I hugged and kissed him through the web of tubes and wires that connected him to the fluids and monitors.

The doctors told us that he had cancer of the liver, cirrhosis, and hepatitis C, probably from a transfusion during one of his baseball surgeries, and now dormant. This information the doctors released to the press the next day, along with the news that he needed a liver transplant and that without one he could survive two to four weeks.

In this disclosure, his doctors made an ethical compromise. That is, they lied out of respect for his privacy. He did not want people to feel pity for him. He did not want them watching the clock and guessing when he would die.

In fact, Mickey was already sinking into a coma. Without a transplant he might not live another forty-eight hours.

The compassion of the physicians led to some of the debate over how quickly Mick received a donor organ. The public wasn't told how desperate his condition really was. The tumor was blocking his bile duct, and his stomach was swollen from bacteria and pus. He was badly jaundiced and the liver failure was shutting down his kidneys.

The family kept up the fiction that, while his case was grave, we remained hopeful. If he received an organ in two weeks or a month, we said, we were confident he would recover.

Much was later made of the fact that the typical wait for a liver transplant is 130 days. But in Texas, which is served in part by the Southwest Organ Bank, the average waiting time for a patient as critically ill as Mick was 3.3 days.

He was in his second day on the list when a liver, blood type O, became available. Mick was blood type O. As a family, we were too busy feeling thrilled and grateful to worry about whether a controversy would develop. We thought it was a miracle, not an ethical dilemma.

Of course, the doctors were aware that they would be the targets of some merciless second-guessing. Dr. Goran Klintmalm, the head of the Baylor Transplant Institute, said later that his first reaction was, "Oh, no. Let us see if we can do someone else and let him wait for a few days so people can see he is waiting like everyone else.

"But Mick was extraordinarily sick. He was the only one here in North Texas waiting for a liver who was that sick. The donor liver was the right blood group. You cannot ethically deny a patient what may be the only chance he has. You don't know if or when you will get another one. So obviously we did the transplant."

There are other factors: the size of the liver, the proximity of the donor. The liver will begin to decline within twelve hours after being removed.

Of all the tests that were made, none showed that the cancer had spread beyond the liver. The doctors kept another patient on standby in case the biopsy detected any malignant cells in the lymph nodes. The tests showed no cancer in the cells. Mick received his new liver. (The standby patient received one a day or so later.)

I can't pretend to understand the medical language, much less the decision making. I can only repeat what we were told and learned: The same night Mick underwent his transplant, a doctor at the New York University Medical Center was offered an organ from Texas. What did it mean?

Dr. Lewis Tepperman, the head of NYU liver transplant program, said it meant that no qualified patient in the state of Texas had been bypassed. "It was kosher," he added, referring to the decision. Mick, with his classic, white Anglo-Saxon Protestant face, would have smiled at his choice of words.

At around 4:00 on the morning of June 8, Mickey was wheeled into the operating room. He was nearly in a coma, sedated and feeble. When they started down the hall, he startled the doctors by raising his head slightly and saying, "Good. Let's get it done." That ought to tell you about the strength of his will, and the fight in him, even when he was almost unconscious.

The surgery itself was performed by Dr. Robert Goldstein,

who wore his hair in a ponytail. I'm not sure why, but Danny, David, Mick Jr., and I found that sign of independence reassuring. But then, we were fond of all the doctors.

I need to admit right here that I have relied on the experts for this account of what happened. I wasn't in the room. I wouldn't know what I had seen if I had been.

The operation lasted more than six hours. They first had to probe for signs the cancer had spread. At that point, they found none. Mick had had his gallbladder removed several years earlier, and next they had to hack through a lot of scar tissue. They found a liver that was hard, lumpy, and swollen. The bile duct was blocked and it took painstaking minutes to drain all the pus that had formed there.

I thought about the five days that Mick had put himself to bed before he went to the hospital. He must have been in agony.

Only after they had removed the diseased liver did the doctors find microscopic evidence that some cancer cells were present in the blood vessels around the bile duct. It was their first hint that the prognosis would not be as favorable as they—and the Mantles—had hoped.

The medical team had made all the tests, done all the screening. There was nothing they could have tried that would have caused them to stop the operation and save the liver for someone else.

By midafternoon on the 8th, it appeared that a miracle was indeed taking place. At 3:30 P.M., Mickey's eyes flickered. Dr. Klintmalm leaned over him and said, "Hi, Mickey. How are you?" He closed his eyes and went back to sleep.

But by the time the doctors appeared at a press conference, still in their green scrubs, his new liver was functioning, his kidneys were working, and his jaundice had been reduced by 70 percent.

Immediately, the pointed questions started coming: Had Mickey Mantle received special treatment because of his celebrity status? Is it fair to donate organs as scarce as a liver to someone whose drinking may have ruined his own?

In this debate, care needs to be taken not to lose the lesson of Mick's story: You can't solve a problem by looking at it through the bottom of a bottle. But the medical opinion was undecided. His cancer could have been caused by the hepatitis virus. "That isn't lifestyle," said another of his doctors, Kent Hamilton. "That is bad luck. The alcohol and the hepatitis [together] were a witch's brew."

Dr. Klintmalm quoted Baylor's policy of not providing a transplant to an alcoholic unless he could prove he had stopped drinking for at least six months. Mick had been sober for a year and a half and it was documented. "This was a man who had abused alcohol," he said, "and who understood what was wrong."

He posed a question in return: If you make medical decisions on the basis of moral judgments, where do you stop? Do you deny extraordinary care to a patient crippled in a car accident because he or she was speeding? Do you deny a cancer patient because he or she smoked, or heart patients who never exercised?

"In this society," he said, "we forgive people who have sinned."

Based on the outpouring of letters and calls from around the country, we know that this is true. On the whole, society forgives, but the body doesn't. Mick waited too late to heal these injuries, but, oh, what a fine example of dignity, pride, and bravery he left us as he accepted this verdict.

To those with loved ones who did not receive a donor organ, and to the few critics who won't believe the system worked, I can only say this:

Thousands will live because Mickey Mantle died. This is the truth of what happened in August 1995. This is the bottom line. This is what the doctors say and what I believe now and always. The future will leave no doubt. The organ donor networks used to count their responses by the tens. Now, they count them by the thousands. It does not stretch the facts to say that this increase in the public's awareness was due to Mick's transplant, even though in the end it could not save him.

Through the Mickey Mantle Foundation, organ donor cards were distributed in every major league stadium. They were designed on the front to look like his baseball cards. Mick had hoped to announce the campaign himself at The Ballpark in Arlington in late August.

At first, I don't think any of us, except Roy True, heard the fears the doctors were confiding. We were listening more closely when Dr. Goldstein said, "It will be very difficult for him, but I feel comfortable that he will survive."

We took heart from the numbers: At Baylor, 85 percent of their transplant patients lived at least one year; 70 percent lived for five. And this was Mickey Mantle, who had been fast and strong and invincible when he was young, and who specialized in ninth-inning rallies.

By Friday the ninth, Mick was awake, smiling, and had a one-word answer for how he felt and what his doctors had accomplished:

"Incredible."

They had left a drain in his abdomen. I wouldn't even try to guess how many bottles of fluids they had filled. But I told him, and I was only half teasing, "Gosh, your stomach is so small. I haven't seen your stomach that flat since you were twenty years old."

That same morning they wheeled him back into the operating room to remove the drain and to stop some bleeding around the new liver. Dr. Goldstein said the problem was minor and had been easily corrected. He was still in intensive care, but off the respirator that had controlled his breathing.

I was elected to represent the family at an afternoon press conference with the medical team. I couldn't keep the tears out of my eyes. "We just feel it was a miracle that he got this liver so soon," I said. "He was going downhill very fast. He was dying. We're very grateful to the donor family."

Dr. K. elaborated: "What we would have seen if we had not found a liver for him is that Mr. Mantle would have suddenly—maybe by today or tomorrow or Sunday—would have started taking a turn for the worse in a very nasty way."

David and Danny took over the job of acting as spokesmen for the family, returning calls, keeping the media and his former teammates informed. It wasn't a job that Mickey Jr., the shyest of the three, had a desire to share. After Mick was transferred from intensive care, they took turns spending the night in his rooms, sleeping on the foldout couch in the parlor.

I think each of them secretly enjoyed being able to give orders to his dad when Dad couldn't always talk back. "There will be some changes in your life you will have to get accustomed to," said David. "You're going to have to calm down a little." They let him know that the three of them would be around to remind him to take his medicine.

His sons wanted to talk to him about retiring, period, and taking life easier. But for now it would be enough if he agreed to just slow down. They had already canceled four or five card show appearances. "I don't think he needs to be out there traveling that much again," said David. "He can relax and enjoy life and start over."

We had sweet pictures in our minds of Mick spending time with Junior's and David's little girls, Mallory and Marilyn, and with the grandson Danny and Kay were expecting, William Charles.

On Saturday, he was able to hobble from his bed to the bathroom and to a chair. He watched some baseball on television with his sons; a good sign, if you think baseball is good therapy.

The doctors were very direct with us about Mick's treatment. During the surgery, they had started him on anti-rejection drugs for his liver and high doses of chemotherapy for his cancer. The risk was hard to miss: The drugs that help the body accept the liver also make the cancer cells grow more quickly.

The threat of rejection is strongest in the first eight weeks, and so this was our immediate concern. Mick's concern was getting home. Hospitals made him stir-crazy, even when he was just a visitor.

The treatments continued and each day he would exercise by taking small steps around his room. Nothing helped his morale more than the expressions of support that kept coming in from his friends in baseball.

Henry Aaron spoke to the graduating class at Harvard, and asked them to pray for "a very dear friend." Aaron added, "Mickey meant an awful lot to me. He was a tremendous athlete. But more than that, he was a tremendous person. People didn't understand him the way they should have. He played eighteen years on one leg."

Friends kept sending us clippings of stories about Mick, and I was amazed that he was still a hero to so many of the current players. They said they were praying for him, rooting for him.

Buck Showalter, who was then the manager of the Yankees, told a writer, Mark Kriegel, about an old-timers' game a few years ago. There was a knock at his door, and when he opened it, there stood Mickey Mantle. They had never met.

According to Buck, it was getting crowded in the clubhouse and Mick asked if he could dress in the manager's office. Showalter said, "Sure, I'll leave."

And Mick said, "No, stay, I want to talk to you some."

"Then I realized," said Buck, "that Mickey Mantle still followed us. And that's when I knew what kind of special job I had." He remembered when he was five or six years old, watching Mick and the Yankees on television. "He was my hero. He was the blond, switch-hitting center fielder for the New York Yankees. That was something we all wanted to be. A lot of us lived our dreams through him."

Mick reacted like a kid when he received a baseball in a glass case, autographed by all of the 1995 New York Yankees. He was only vaguely aware, in the beginning, of the suspicions that his transplant had resulted from special treatment. The whole family appreciated Mike Lupica's tart reply to the charge on ESPN: "Get a life. The guy was going to die."

One month after he entered the hospital, Mick was discharged on Wednesday, June 28, and went home with Danny and Kay. When he heard about the accusations, he could not resist joining in. He told a writer from the *New York Daily News*, "People think I got that liver because of who I am, but they have rules they go by. They told me I had one day to live. If I hadn't got this one, I wouldn't have made it."

As an outpatient, Mick returned to the hospital for a chemotherapy treatment and then for a blood transfusion, the first of seven. The chemo had led to anemia and his weight had dropped to 170 pounds—he weighed 208 the day he was admitted. He was having good and bad days. During this time, Roy True told a reporter, "He is in a very reflective mood. In all the years I've known him, I have never seen him think so hard about life."

He had been besieged with requests from the media, and on July 11, he appeared with his doctors at a press conference to take their questions. He looked pale and shrunken, and the brim of his baseball cap came down to his eyes and ears. The reporters thought the chemo had caused his hair to fall out, until he ran his hand through his fine blond locks. But the cap did seem too large for his head.

His walk was stiff and when he sat down I wondered if he was up for this. But he did what he had done so often in his life—he rose to the occasion. He said the right things, and he said them with humor and honesty.

"I owe so much to God and the American people," he said. "I'm going to spend the rest of my life trying to make it up. It seems to me like all I've done is take. Have fun and take. I'm going to start giving something back."

You could hear an occasional break in his voice, but you saw the emotion in the faces of those who were watching, too. He hadn't been a taker. But you knew what he meant. He felt lucky because he got to do the one thing he was good at, and be paid for it. The last few years, he felt guilty about the money he made for signing his name, but part of that money was funding the Mickey Mantle Foundation, so he was already giving something back. He had other obligations in mind, too.

"I'd like to say to kids out there, if you're looking for a role model, *this* is a role model." His thumb was pointing at his chest. With a thin smile, he said, "Don't be like me.

"God gave me a body and an ability to play baseball," he went on. "God gave me everything and I just . . ." He couldn't finish the sentence. He made a throwaway gesture with one hand.

He was wearing a cap from the All-Star Game, played at Arlington that month, and he became visibly more assured as the reporters responded to his remarks. When he was asked if he had signed one of the organ donor cards he was now promoting, he said, in all seriousness, "I don't have anything good to give. Everything I've got is worn out. Although I've heard people say they'd like to have my heart . . . it's never been used."

His quips were still aimed mostly at himself. He was still unforgiving of his own faults. I think this is part of what endeared him to so many fans. But if you win three Most Valuable Player awards, lead the league in home runs four times, make it to the Hall of Fame, and play in twelve World Series, I doubt that many people would feel you threw your talent away.

The only time Mick got snappish was when someone brought up the issue of special treatment. "They're going to answer that for you," he said, pointing to Dr. Bob Goldstein, the surgeon who did his transplant.

Dr. Goldstein repeated the criteria and the policies that were followed, and tried to put it to rest. I don't know if anyone ever will. But months later, a report from the United Network for Organ Sharing reviewed the case and said all the procedures in Mick's case were correct. A computer in Richmond, Virginia, had made the match, and there was no way to rig the computer.

"Hopefully," said Dr. Goldstein, "Mickey can become an example of someone . . . who has been given a second chance."

The next day he learned that his X rays had detected spots on his lungs. The cancer had spread. They talked about increasing the chemotherapy. Mick asked the doctors not to release this newest development. His second chance was not going to be a long one.

Then the stomach pains came back.

On July 28, two months to the day after David had dropped him off at the front door, he checked back into

Baylor Medical. The rumors were so persistent that he had to address them. But this time he was too sick to appear in person. He had promised an interview to the ABC show *Good Morning, America,* and he videotaped a statement that ran on the air on August 1.

In the tape, he said, "Hi, this is Mick. When I left Baylor University Medical Center about a month ago, I felt great. I have been [coming back] to the hospital for checkups every once in a while and, about two weeks ago, the doctors found a couple of spots of cancer in my lungs.

"Now I'm taking chemotherapy to get rid of the new cancer. I hope to get back to feeling as good as when I first left here. . . .

"If you'd like to do something really great, be a donor."

You could draw a straight line through Mickey's chart. It was as if the calendar was trying to tell us something. He had entered the hospital on the 28th of May, went home on the 28th of June, and was readmitted on the 28th of July. The newspapers the next day quoted various medical experts as giving him six to eighteen months to live.

The family knew what the outsiders didn't. I knew Mick was down to his final days, even though he asked the doctors not to tell me. Roy True was in the room with our sons when Dr. Goldstein gave him the grim news.

He said there were "complications," spots on the lung. "At first," said Roy, "Mick looked up like he was surprised. And then he said simply, very simply, 'Well, let's just fix it like you did the other thing.'"

The other thing, of course, was the transplant that replaced his diseased liver.

"It was kind of weird," Roy reflected. "Everything

seemed to hinge on the liver, and there was no rejection at all. Now he had regained a little weight, was doing about fifteen minutes on the treadmill. He couldn't stop talking about going out to play golf again."

Then there were the plans, so many plans. He had already laid out his idea for an organ donor awareness program at Baylor. It was to be called Mickey's Team. He thought of the slogan himself: "Be a hero, be a donor." He was going to tape a series of public service announcements.

The suddenness of his setback, and the reality that his time was running out, cheated us of a final intimacy. Each of our sons had a memory, or two, of acting in shifts to be with their dad around the clock. There is no point in my repeating them here.

But I do feel a need to correct a wrong impression left by news stories about Mick's last days. This isn't meant as a slap at the media. Over the years they have been wonderful to the Mantles, and protected Mick even when it might have helped more if they hadn't.

But the references to our sons too often made it appear that they were estranged from their father, that there were unhealed wounds between them. He faulted himself so often about being gone, about not being there for them, that may have been an easy conclusion to draw. But absence isn't the same as neglect.

He called them nearly every day. Their pride in him, and their love for him, was never in doubt. He taught them to be generous, which is not a little thing, and to help others, especially the helpless.

They didn't have any fences to mend in the last year or so. They just opened the gate a lot wider.

I do think our lives would have been very different if he had survived. He had reached a point where he wanted more time with us as a family. He was returning to an old-fashioned idea of what was important. We still spent holidays together, our anniversaries and birthdays—me and Mick and the boys. He wanted it that way.

We were never really apart, even though we lived in separate houses. We were both sober now, able to stand back and look clearly at the damage of our lives. And still there was love. Our whole family was on the road to recovery. I think, in time, that Mick and I would have been under the same roof again.

He had all the money he or his children would ever need. He didn't have to travel anymore, or take his drinking with him, because he no longer had to run from his demons.

He told me about the last of these as we watched television one night, after dinner, a year before he died. He had kept a secret to himself for nearly his entire life and for the forty-three years we were married.

I have wrestled with myself, have gone back and forth, about whether to reveal it now. I decided I would because this was one of the lessons of our sobriety, that you are never alone, that even the most successful among us can feel lost or worthless. Even the manliest of men can have bad things happen to them.

In the end, I decided that what Mickey revealed was crucial to understanding those parts of his life that were the least flattering to him.

I no longer recall the name of the movie, or who the

stars were, but the story was about child abuse and the conflicts that grew out of it.

Quietly, unemotionally, as if talking about someone else, Mick said, "That happened to me."

I asked him what he meant. Exactly what had happened?

He then told me how, when he was four or five years old, a half-sister, who was then in her late teens, molested him. She toyed with him sexually. She would pull down his pants and play with him, usually as a few of her friends, teenagers and older, watched. At times he would get a tiny erection. He saw the smirking faces and heard the howl of their laughter. He doesn't recall crying. He doesn't know how long they kept him on display. They let him go when they grew tired of the game.

I don't think I am making too much of this. This wasn't the curious innocence of children of a similar age. For a young boy who would grow into a proud and famous man, I can only guess at how humiliated Mick felt. Did it have a lasting effect on him? I only know that he still remembered the details after nearly sixty years. The sexual teasing ended when the half-sister moved away, but I think the shame and confusion stayed deep inside him.

Mick could not stand to be laughed at or ridiculed, ever. I can't analyze the harm this indignity may have caused. But I never thought he respected women. He demonstrated it in the ladies he chose for his one-night stands, in the crude way he talked and acted in front of women when he drank.

And in the way he treated me, with too much credit for

raising our sons and too little for being an adoring and faithful wife.

To my knowledge, he never spoke of this subject before and we never brought it up again. But that night I thought I understood more clearly than I ever had why his ego was so fragile. He was a loner who loved a crowd, when they cheered from a distance.

I wanted so much for the two of us to look with fresh eyes at our life together, and to let Mick see that we had finished strong. We had won. Our sons had dealt with their problems and turned out well. Of my memories, the sweet and happy times outweighed the other kind.

But the doctors could do nothing now but ease his pain, and when he wasn't knocked out on morphine there were relatives and old teammates to see. This was the last pleasure left to him, the reliving of his Yankee years.

Once, when we were alone, I asked him, "Mick, I've written a letter to you. It's not long. May I read it to you?"

I could see him try to shift his weight, and the pain made a fist of his voice. "Oh, honey," he said. "I'm half asleep right now. Can it wait?"

I said sure, of course, it could wait. But there wouldn't be another chance. Instead of reading the letter to him, I dropped it inside his casket. It wasn't a long letter. I had written that I loved him with all my heart, and always would, and how proud I was to have been Mrs. Mickey Mantle. I told him his sons thought he was a great father, and he should believe it because their opinion was the only one that mattered.

I said he really was a hero. The public decides who is and who isn't, and you can't resign if you don't want to be one. He was a hero now because he had gotten sober and shared his story with other people. When he learned he had cancer, he faced it head-on, with no fear or anger. He was born to be a hero. He had been one all his life.

His Yankee teammates were flying in from around the country to say good-bye. On Wednesday, August 9, Whitey Ford had dropped by for a visit. Moose Skowron, Hank Bauer, Bobby Richardson, and John Blanchard had been in to see him earlier. Dr. DeLarios left the room, not believing his eyes. "I saw a dying man sitting up in bed, talking," he said.

The next day, Dr. DeLarios canceled a chemo session that had been scheduled for Friday. He told Mick the cancer had spread throughout his body. "I'm sorry," he said. "There is nothing else we can do." When he started to tell him how much time he had left, Mick cut him off.

"That was it," recalled Roy True. "Mickey thanked him and acted like he would live for another twenty years."

At thirty minutes after midnight, on the morning of Sunday, the thirteenth of August, he awoke for a brief few seconds and looked at David and me. He held up his hands and we each took one. Forty minutes later, the line on the EKG machine went flat. At that moment, no tears came. I was relieved that he no longer had to suffer or hide his pain from his friends.

It was a sign of how attracted people were to Mick that the doctors took his death nearly as hard as his family. "His disposition was remarkable," said Dr. DeMarco. "Whenever you would disturb him or wake him he would always smile. I have never seen anybody do that."

Dr. Klintmalm praised his fighting spirit. "He fought

very hard," said Dr. K. "I don't know if he got it from base-ball or he was born with it. Mickey wished to live. He had reason to live."

He was dead one month after he had appeared at his televised press conference to discuss his transplant and talk about "giving something back." He already had.

I was left with a sense of unexpressed feelings and so were his sons. After the family viewing the night before the services, we turned to walk out of the mortuary. Danny stopped and went back. He bent down and hugged Mick in the coffin and said, "I know you didn't think you were a good dad, but you were, and I love you." Then he left and caught up with the rest of us.

If anyone wondered what Mickey Mantle meant to the rest of the country, his funeral answered every question. The day—August 15, 1995—passed in a blur for me, a blur of old friends from over the years and the wishes of strangers who had grown up cheering for Number 7.

There were seats for 1,500 inside the sanctuary of the Lovers Lane United Methodist Church in Dallas. Another 1,500 seats in adjoining chapels were linked to the service by a video monitor.

Outside, 2,000 mourners had gathered for the 2:00 P.M. service. Some of them had been waiting since dawn. Some had flown in from New York, Oklahoma, and California, and some had stories to tell. A twenty-six-year-old Dallas man named Christopher Rook remembered being stranded with a flat tire on Christmas Eve of 1993. A limousine pulled up, Rook told George Vecsey of the *New York Times,* and a man asked if he needed help.

Rook said he would manage, and the man asked how

his Christmas shopping was going. Rook said he still needed a present for his father. The man in the limo handed him a hundred-dollar bill.

"Up to the moment he signed it," Rook said as he stood outside the church, "I didn't know who it was. Needless to say, I didn't spend it. It's in a frame in my house."

The pallbearers were all former Yankees: Yogi Berra, Whitey Ford, Skowron, Bauer, Blanchard, and Bobby Murcer, who followed Mickey out of Oklahoma to Yankee Stadium. Other ex-Yankees had made their way to Dallas. Bobby Richardson gave one of the eulogies. From the teams of the fifties had come Jerry Coleman, Eddie Robinson, Andy Carey, and Dr. Bobby Brown, who had a career in medicine and later was president of the American League.

Joe Pepitone, Tony Kubek, and Tom Tresh represented the sixties. Stan Musial of the Cardinals, Mick's boyhood idol, had flown in from St. Louis. The guests included four governors: George Pataki of New York, George W. Bush of Texas, Zell Miller of Georgia, and former Texas governor Ann Richards.

George Steinbrenner sat in one of the front pews, next to Reggie Jackson and Billy Crystal, the actor-comic and lifelong Yankee fan. Billy said that at his Bar Mitzvah, he tried to imitate Mick's Oklahoma twang.

So many people had so many memories, funny, tender, sad, heroic. Some came very close to explaining what made him Mickey Mantle. "I don't think to this day that Mickey realized how much he touched the hearts of fans," said Bobby Murcer. "We truly lost not only an American hero, but a person who portrayed the innocence and honesty that we'd all like to have."

After Mick went public with his drinking problem, he spoke so often of his flaws and regrets that I worried that people would think this was all his life had been. I was so grateful when Bob Costas, in a truly eloquent eulogy, spoke to those feelings. The family had asked Bob to give the main eulogy, not because he kept Mick's baseball card in his wallet, although we loved the idea of that, but because he seemed to sense what was inside the pinstripes:

In a very different time than today, the first baseball commissioner, Kenesaw Mountain Landis, said every boy builds a shrine to some baseball hero, and before that shrine a candle always burns.

For a huge portion of my generation, Mickey Mantle was that baseball hero. And for reasons that no statistics, no dry recitation of facts can possibly capture, he was the most compelling baseball hero of our lifetime. And he was our symbol of baseball at a time when the game meant something to us that perhaps it no longer does.

Mickey Mantle had those dual qualities so seldom seen, exuding dynamism and excitement, but at the same time touching your heart—flawed, wounded. We knew there was something poignant about Mickey Mantle before we knew what poignant meant. We didn't just root for him. We felt for him.

Long before many of us ever cracked a serious book, we knew something about mythology as we watched Mickey Mantle run out a home run through the lengthening shadows of a late Sunday afternoon at Yankee Stadium. . . .

Mick always said that no one on television explained the grip that baseball gets on you better than Bob Costas in his work at NBC. Certainly, on a day when we hungered to hear it, he helped to explain Mick, even to those of us who had lived with him all of our lives

There were heartening words as well from the Reverend William Jennings Bryan III, an unforgettable name, but unrelated to the lawyer and orator, and Bobby Richardson, who retired from baseball to become a lay minister. There were few dry eyes in the church when Roy Clark, the country singer and one of Mick's golfing buddies, sang "Yesterday When I Was Young," keeping a promise made years earlier.

It would be hard to pick out a line and say, "This was the one that was surely based on Mick's life." But it isn't hard to figure why the song was his favorite, with lyrics like these:

> I lived by night and shunned the naked light of day, and
>   only now I see how the years ran away . . .
> I ran so fast that time and youth at last ran out. I never
>   stopped to think what life is all about . . . yesterday
>   when I was young.

Mickey was laid to rest in a crypt next to our son Billy at the Sparkman-Hillcrest cemetery. After the ceremony, there was a reception for our friends and guests at Roy True's home. It wasn't a sad or crying time. I looked around the living room and watched, with fascination, as Yogi Berra chatted with Stan Musial and Bob Costas talked with Billy Crystal.

Someone told me that the funeral had been covered live on national television (on ESPN), and one of the cable channels in New York, the Classic Sports Network, planned to carry an eighteen-hour tribute. It would include highlights of Mick's career, reruns of a documentary, and several interviews, plus Mickey Mantle Day in its entirety, when the Yankees retired his uniform and the cheers wouldn't subside. I felt sort of fortunate that I would not be there to watch.

I thought of the reason Mick gave when he asked the doctors not to release any more details of his illness. He was still trying to watch a baseball game every day, the Texas Rangers in Dallas, the Braves or the Cubs on the superstations. He said he was tired of hearing updates on his condition.

This is how I will remember my husband. When he talked about his failure as a father, or his disappointment at not making the most of his physical gifts, his humility was real. It takes a big man to admit his mistakes. The bigger the mistakes, the bigger the man. He was still heroic. As one writer said, "This was no geek seeking attention on *Geraldo*. This was the Mick."

Epilogue:
The Empty Glass

IN THE PAGES YOU HAVE JUST READ, IT WAS OUR WISH TO share a part of our lives and the effects the disease of alcoholism can have on your life as an individual, as well as on a family unit.

As we look back on some of these anecdotes, there was a time when they were very painful memories, but through the healing of recovery we can now see humor in them. It would not be fair to blame all of our ups and downs on alcoholism. Life is never a straight line, but we hope to make others more aware of the role alcoholism can play by making everyday ups and downs more traumatic.

Though all of us share the disease, it may cause a lot of different reactions for each of us. Yet we all seem to experience similar feelings, such as depression, loneliness, and low self-esteem. We were always a family that stayed close together and kept in touch daily. We talked often, but never really shared our deeper feelings. Actions such as these led to a sense of isolation, even though we were surrounded by the people we loved.

In the pages of this book, we have tried to convey how, through alcoholism, our vision was clouded regarding what was really happening in our lives. We were lost in an empty existence and did not know how to live in the real world. For some of us, the drinking was so familiar or normal that it felt comfortable. We even lied to ourselves, saying this was how everyone lived. It's a very scary thing to wake up to the realization that life is passing you by and you don't remember a good portion of it.

Change takes a lot of courage and a lot of faith. We had tried as individuals many times to stop drinking on our own, only to realize how powerless we were by ourselves, unable to control our own lives. We all need something, or someone, more powerful than the disease and ourselves. That is part of what we learned in a twelve-step recovery program. You have to turn some things over to a higher power, and, for our family, that higher power is God.

Alcohol is a cunning disease. It throws a cloak over our spirit and belittles us, although at the time we were drinking we felt just the opposite—we were living a lie. When the drinks are gone, you are once again alone and afraid.

Continuing the same behavior but expecting different results is just unrealistic. With this cycle comes regret, which leads right into alcohol depression. With recovery through a twelve-step program, our family has learned that reliving our mistakes instead of learning from them can be a discouraging and deadly direction to take. Even though

Mick got sober late, he did not regret the gift and the difference it made in his own life, even though it turned out to be such a short period of time. He did reflect on the times he wished he would have done certain things differently, but he quickly changed direction. He started to use his new life in such a positive way, to move forward and not drown in an unchangeable past.

As a result of Mick's celebrity status, he was able to make an impact on the public's attention to the need for organ donors. The Mickey Mantle Foundation was formed by Mick to promote organ donor awareness. He also began a new relationship with his sons, on a level of respect and encouragement, no longer as just drinking buddies.

Never let your age, or the thought of there being too much past to overcome, discourage you. Sobriety for our family was the gift of life, through which we are not afraid to share our feelings and we don't have to feel alone anymore. Sobriety will never take away life's conflicts, but it gave our family the ability to deal with them.

We hope that you as readers may find the courage to take the steps our family took, if you find your life plagued by the disease of alcoholism. For those of you who are fortunate enough not to be touched by this disease, we plead with you to not be judgmental, for alcoholism is not a weakness, it is an illness that can be treated.

This was one of the lessons we drew from Mick's life, heroic in his youth and, again, in his death.

THE MANTLES—MERLYN, MICKEY JR., DAVID AND MARLA, DANNY AND KAY

Index

Index

Index

INDEX

INDEX